The Americas

Ancient Civilizations of
The Americas

Antony Mason

Dorling Kindersley

London, New York, Sydney, Delhi,
Paris, Munich, and Johannesburg

Publisher: Sean Moore
Editorial Director: Chuck Wills
Project Editor: Barbara Minton
Art Director: Dirk Kaufman
Production Director: David Proffit

Ancient Civilizations of the
Americas
0-7894-7831-5

First US edition 2001
Published in the US by
DK Publishing, Inc.
95 Madison Avenue
New York, New York 10016

First published 2001 by
BBC Worldwide Ltd.
Woodlands, 80 Wood Lane,
London W12 0TT

Produced for BBC Worldwide by
Toucan Books, Ltd. London

Cover photograph: Werner
Forman Archive

Printed and bound in France by
Imprinerie Pollina s.a.
N 80762-C

Color separations by
Imprinerie Pollina s.a.

PICTURE CREDITS:

Page 2 South American Pictures.
6 Still Pictures. 9 Olive Pearson.
10 Warren Morgan. 11 Chris
Forsey. 12-13 Michael Freeman.
14 Werner Forman Archive.
15 South American Pictures.
16 Chris Forsey. 17 South
American Pictures/Chris Sharp.
18-19, 20 Robert Harding.
21 David Bernstein, New
York/Werner Forman, B; Private
Collection/Werner Forman, T.
22 Museo Amano, Lima/The
Art Archive. 23 Hutchison
Library/H.R. Dorig, T; South
American Pictures, R. 24 Trip/
M Barlow. 27-8 Robert Harding.
28-9 Chris Forsey.
30-1 Trip/ R Powers. 31-2
Michael Freeman. 33 Jurgen
Liepe. 35 British Museum/
Michael Holford, T; Robert
Harding/Robert Frerck, B.
36 AKG/Veintimilla. 37 South
American Pictures. 38 Chris
Forsey,T; Field Museum of
Natural History, Chicago/
Werner Forman Archive, B.
38-9 Robert Harding. 40 Michael
Holford. 43 Robert
Harding/Doug Traverso.
44 British Museum/Werner
Forman Archive. 45 British
Museum/Michael Holford. 46
The Art Archive. 47 Staatliche
Museum, Berlin/BPK. 48 Trip/M.
Barlow, T; BPK , B. 49 South
American Pictures/Kimball
Morrison. 50 Hutchison Library.
51 Museum fur Volkerkunde/
BPK. 52 Chris Forsey. 53 C.M.
Dixon. 54-5 Trip/M. Barlow.
56 Chris Forsey. 57 Michael
Freeman. 58 Michael Holford.
59 Robert Harding. 60 Michael
Freeman. 63 Olive Pearson. 64
South American Pictures/Tony
Morrison. 65 Trip/H. Rogers, T;
National Archives, Mexico
City/The Art Archive, B. 66
The Art Archive. 67 Hutchison
Library. 68 Anthropological
Museum, Mexico City/Michael
Holford, T; British Museum/
Michael Holford, B. 69 AKG.
70 Robert Harding. 71 Olive
Pearson. 72 Robert Harding/
Robert Frerck. 73 Staatliche
Museum, Berlin/BPK. 74-5
The Art Archive. 76 Hutchison
Library. 77 Hutchison Library,
L; Chris Forsey, R. 78
Montezuma, Last King of the Aztecs
by unknown artist/Pitti Palace,
Florence/The Art Archive.
81 *Christopher Columbus
Disembarking in America* by
Dioscuro de la Puebla/The Art
Archive. 82-3 The Art Archive.
84 Staatsbibliothek, Berlin
/BPK. 85 *Hernando
Cortez*, anonymous portrait/
Accademia Real de San
Fernando, Madrid/BPK. 86
Francisco Pizarro by Daniel Diaz
Vazquez/The Art Archive. 87
Robert Harding/Robert Frerck.
88 Museo del Oro, Lima/Robert
Harding/Robert Frerck. 89 New
York Public Library/The Art
Archive. 90 Michael Holford.
90-1 The Art Archive. 92 BPK.
93 Bettman/Corbis.

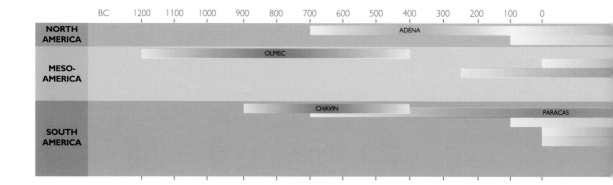

Contents

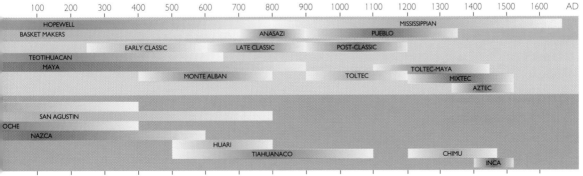

| 100 | 200 | 300 | 400 | 500 | 600 | 700 | 800 | 900 | 1000 | 1100 | 1200 | 1300 | 1400 | 1500 | 1600 | AD |

HOPEWELL
BASKET MAKERS
ANASAZI
PUEBLO
MISSISSIPPIAN
EARLY CLASSIC
LATE CLASSIC
POST-CLASSIC
TEOTIHUACAN
MAYA
MONTE ALBAN
TOLTEC
TOLTEC-MAYA
MIXTEC
AZTEC
SAN AGUSTIN
OCHE
NAZCA
HUARI
TIAHUANACO
CHIMU
INCA

A NEW WORLD

1 A NEW WORLD

The history of civilization is skewed towards the peoples who left a legacy in monuments and artefacts. Successful, stable societies that make little lasting impression on the landscape receive far less attention. Nowhere is this more clearly demonstrated than in the Americas, where a series of magnificent civilizations has stolen the limelight.

The dazzling treasures of the Aztecs and Inca amazed the Spanish conquistadores when they arrived in the Americas in the 16th century, and have overshadowed many of the remarkable cultures that preceded and contributed to them, or developed alongside them. What drove the peoples of the Americas to their great achievements begs questions about the very nature of civilization – all the more fascinating because both North and South America stood at virtually the same starting point about 10,000 years ago.

Previous page: Lake Pehoe and the Paine Horns mountains in the Torres del Paine region of southern Chile.

THE FIRST AMERICANS

No remains of human species earlier than our modern form, *Homo sapiens*, have been found in the Americas, so the generally accepted view is that all the peoples of both North and South America are descended from comparatively recent migrants. The traditional theory is that Stone Age hunter-gatherers from Siberia arrived by crossing the Bering Strait some 15,000–20,000 years ago. This would have been during the last Ice Age, when a vast ice sheet up to 3 km (2 miles) thick covered Canada and half of the USA, the North Atlantic and northern Europe. So much water was locked into this ice sheet that the sea level dropped 60 m (200 ft) or more. Today, the waters of the Bering Strait are only 50 m (160 ft) deep; during the Ice Age, the land was exposed to form a broad 'land bridge' (called Beringia), linking Asia with North America.

Clovis and other theories

During the 1920s and 1930s, weapons of flaked flint were found at sites in New Mexico, USA, called Folsom and Clovis. These were very sharp projectile 'points', or spearheads, that had been strapped to wooden shafts. What made the Clovis points particularly fascinating was the fact that they were found among the bones of extinct animals, such as mammoths and the giant bison, which died

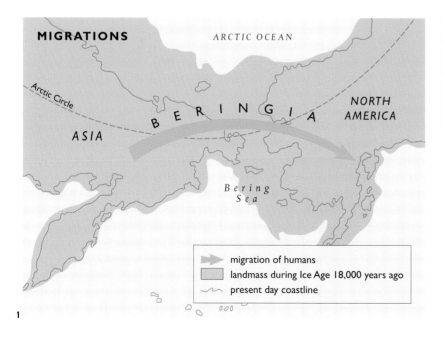

1. During the last Ice Age a land bridge called Beringia linked Asia with North America. It is thought that the first settlers crossed from Siberia around 18,000 years ago.

MIGRATIONS

ARCTIC OCEAN

Arctic Circle

ASIA

B E R I N G I A

NORTH AMERICA

Bering Sea

migration of humans
landmass during Ice Age 18,000 years ago
present day coastline

out over 10,000 years ago. This was the first evidence that the early Americans dated back so far.

Since then, Clovis-style points have been found across North America, and also in Mesoamerica (Mexico and Central America). Radio-carbon dating of surrounding material has confirmed dates of 9500–11,500 years ago. On the basis of this evidence, it seemed likely that these first migrants had come to Alaska 14,000–20,000 years ago, and then slipped southwards through a corridor in the ice sheet that appeared during a brief warming spell between 13,000 and 12,000 years ago.

But this neat theory was torpedoed by a series of discoveries in South America beginning in the 1970s. At Monte Verde in southern Chile, in particular, a wide range of artefacts – including stone weapons, the remains of tent poles and even medicinal herbs – were found preserved in peat. They dated to at least 14,000 years ago. If the first Americans had come south of the ice sheet before 13,000 years ago, the horizon for their arrival could stretch back to 40,000 or 50,000 years ago.

Meanwhile, linguists concluded that the variety of languages of the Americas could not possibly have come from one ancestral source. Studies of skull shapes from Palaeo-Indian (or Stone Age) sites suggested an ancestry related to Polynesians, or the prehistoric peoples of Japan, as well as non-Asian sources. And DNA tests have pointed to links not only with Siberians and Japanese, but also Europeans, who may have reached America by eastward migration through Asia – or by working their way around the Atlantic ice sheets in boats. Today, the most favoured theory still focuses on

1

migration through Beringia. But this could have taken place in a trickle effect between about 10,000 and 50,000 years ago, with some groups advancing to the south of the great ice sheet well before the temporary thaw around 12,000 years ago. More important, perhaps, is the fact that after about 8000 BC, no further migrants arrived, and it appears that the Americas remained effectively isolated from the rest of the world for the next 9500 years.

Hunting and gathering

One set of migrants stayed in the far north. At first they hunted among coastal woodlands of Alaska, but after about 2500 years ago, some groups moved eastwards into the tundra and began to live entirely by hunting and fishing sea creatures in the frozen wastes of the Arctic Circle. These were the ancestors of the Inuit (Eskimo) peoples. At the end of the last Ice Age, the landscape of North America was very different from today's. Essentially, the bands of climatic regions, from tundra through subarctic forests to grasslands, have shifted northwards. The now-arid regions of the southwest – such as Arizona, home to the Clovis and Folsom hunters – were covered in grasslands that

2

1. Chipped from very hard stone such as flint, chalcedony or quartz, Clovis points remain as razor-sharp today as they were when fashioned some 12,000 years ago.

2. Mammoth hunting with Clovis points. In some cases hunters felled their prey by driving them over cliffs.

▶ THE MAMMOTH HUNTERS

Two species of mammoth roamed the vast open spaces of North America during the last Ice Age around 18,000 years ago: the woolly mammoth, which ranged right across the northern landmasses of the world, and the Columbian mammoth, which occurred only in America. Both died out about 11,000 years ago – 500 years after the emergence of hunters who used Clovis points. Were these hunters responsible for their extinction? There is no doubt that the hunters did kill mammoths. Clovis points have been found with mammoth bones, but how they overwhelmed such an enormous animal, 3.4 m (11 ft) high and weighing 6 tonnes, is not clear. They may have operated in teams, perhaps driving herds of mammoths over cliffs or into pit traps, then finishing them off when wounded or constrained. But a greater threat to mammoths was the changing environment. After the last Ice Age, new kinds of grasslands and forest replaced the mixed vegetation that supplied the mammoth's diet. Mammoths were probably heading for extinction – but human hunters may well have hastened the process.

supported a wide range of animal life. This included many now-extinct species, such as the mammoths, giant ground sloths, the very large dire wolf and the native American horse. As the ice sheet retreated, these large mammals were unable to cope with the climate change, and so died out. At this point, it appears, the hunters adopted lighter, more delicate stone weapons, like those found at Folsom, as they switched to smaller prey, such as deer and hares. They also gathered nuts, berries and fruits, fished in the rivers and on the coasts, and collected shellfish.

This kind of lifestyle spread right through both American continents, as far south as Tierra del Fuego, on the southernmost tip of South America. The hunters and gatherers adapted to whatever food was available in their region, often living in small bands that moved in a regular circuit, following the natural patterns of the animals and plants that provided their food. This proved an enduring way of life for many groups. There are still some peoples of the Amazon rain forest who maintain this way of life to this day.

★ North and South America are 13,000 km (7800 miles) from tip to toe. Migrants could have crossed both continents in 1000 years by moving just 25 km (15 miles) a year.

1

SETTLING DOWN

Some bands of hunter-gatherers found they could divide their time between just two seasonal locations, and returned regularly to the same camps, forming semi-permanent settlements. The very first villages in the Americas, it now seems, may have been established as long as 13,000 years ago on the coast of Peru, where settlers exploited year-round supplies of shellfish. Later, hunter-gatherers also found that they could create a more reliable source of food by planting seeds and domesticating animals. Tools altered: heavy mortars and pestles were made for grinding seeds and other plant foods, and could be left permanently at harvest sites. The people of the Cochise culture of south-eastern Arizona were grinding grain with millstones by 5000 BC. Stone axes and adzes were used for woodworking. Long-distance trade routes were forged in this so-called 'archaic' period of transition. Trade in tools and precious hard stones, such as obsidian, spanned considerable distances. Much-prized decorative

1. Rock engraving at Three Rivers, New Mexico. These engravings are thought to illustrate mammoths or mastodons.

seashells from the Gulf of Mexico were traded as far north as the Great Lakes in North America.

By about 5000 BC, seasonal settlers in the highlands of Mesoamerica were growing squash (vegetable marrow), avocado, beans, a kind of grain called amaranth, chillies and – most important of all – a primitive form of maize. In the hotter, more humid lowlands of Mexico the main staple was the root crop manioc, or cassava, although maize was introduced in about 2000 BC. Turkeys and dogs

were raised for food. In the Andes of Peru, agriculture began in about 6500 BC. At first it was limited to crops such as gourds and a native grain called quinoa. Later, the range of crops extended to maize, squash, beans, potatoes and cotton. Early farmers in South America raised guinea pigs for food, and llamas and alpacas for food and wool. Llamas were also domesticated as beasts of burden – the only pack animal of the ancient Americas. Dogs were kept for hunting, and for the table.

THE WONDER OF MAIZE

If the civilizations of the Americas were built on agriculture, then maize was the foundation stone. The immense productivity of this crop gave the peoples of North and South America a security in food supplies that permitted them to turn their minds from farming to cultural and religious pursuits. The origins of maize are uncertain. Maize cultivation is thought to have begun in the highlands of Mexico as early as 5000 BC. Over 1000 years, wild grass strains were progressively hybridized (cross-bred), perhaps with teosinte grass, to produce larger kernels and ears. From an original seed head 3 cm (1 1/4 in) long, it was extended and fattened to 15 cm (6 in). By 2000 BC, maize had been modified sufficiently to produce yields that could support settled communities. Maize crops could be dried and stored. The kernels were then ground by hand using a rectangular slab known today as a metate, and an oblong hand-stone called a mano. The flour was used to make porridge, tortilla pancakes or tamales.

1

1. Maize played such a vital role in American cultures that it was ascribed god-like, supernatural characteristics, as portrayed in pottery from the Moche culture of Peru (AD 100–600).

2. Female 'Venus' figurines, perhaps associated with a fertility cult, are among the most striking examples of the early pottery from Valdivía, Ecuador, dating back to at least 2400 BC.

Village life

As farming took over as a way of life, villages developed. The first pottery was produced around the mouth of the Amazon and on the Caribbean coast of Colombia as early as 4000 BC; by 2400 BC it was also being made at Valdivía on the coast of Ecuador. It reached Peru by about 1750 BC, a development that coincided with the introduction of the heddle loom for weaving textiles in cotton and llama wool. Basketry was another craft that was well advanced in both North and South America by this time. Gold-working, using the basic technique of beating out sheets called 'cold hammering', began in the Andes in around 2100 BC. Copper-working developed around the Great Lakes of North America about the same time, and copper products were traded as far south as Florida.

Trade was a key factor in the spread of cultural change and the techniques of agriculture and manufacture over the passing millennia. It is witnessed, for example, in the presence in Meso-american sites of spondylus shells, which were native to Ecuador and were held to have sacred significance. Trade may also have been a factor in the production of the most sophisticated early pottery of Mesoamerica, which came from the Pacific coast. The Barra and Ocós cultures of 1600 and 1500 BC produced wares and figurines with many similarities to the pottery of the coast of Ecuador. It is possible that early trading links were conducted along the coast.

Hunters and gatherers tend to live in fairly egalitarian groups, with flexible social structures

2

that allow them to form, splinter and regroup at will. Villages and the agricultural life often require greater social control, to organize defence, for example, or – in arid regions – to manage the distribution of water for irrigation. So, along with a more settled existence came the development of social hierarchies, and a distinction between rich and poor, the rulers and the ruled. This is reflected in burial sites, where the richness and quantity of accompanying grave goods clearly separates members of the élite from the crowd. Political power became closely related to religious beliefs. Leaders were linked to deities, and were believed to act as a conduit for their will.

All across the Americas, centres of religious and political authority had large burial mounds, which doubled as temples. A large mound at Indian Knoll, Kentucky, dates from 3000 BC. One of the most impressive early 'mound cities' developed at Poverty Point, Louisiana, and this consisted of a series of symmetrically arranged concentric earthworks. By 1000 BC, the city had a population of 5000.

TIME ON THEIR HANDS

By the 2nd millennium BC, development across the Americas was taking place at hugely varying speeds, depending on the local climate, vegetation and lifestyle. In North America, many groups continued a semi-nomadic existence of hunting and gathering, perhaps with seasonal agriculture. Others settled into villages, and developed more cohesive tribal units and hierarchies. But in Mesoamerica and the Andes, some cultures were beginning to create sophisticated urban societies and the first proper cities of the Americas.

The first major American civilization emerged in the hot and humid lowlands lining the Gulf of Mexico, where silt-rich riverbanks provide some of the region's most fertile soil. This was the land of the Olmecs, who built a series of orderly ceremonial centres and accompanying towns on low hills that rise above the swampy plains. The city of San Lorenzo was the first to dominate, from about 1200 BC. At its centre was a set of rectangular

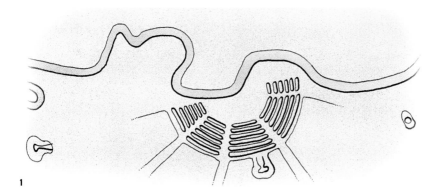

1

1. The semi-circular earthworks at Poverty Point, Louisiana, were raised between 1500 and 700 BC.

2. The largest of the Olmec heads from San Lorenzo stands nearly 3 m (10 ft) tall. Flecks of colour found on some heads suggest that they were painted.

temple platforms and pyramid mounds, the construction of which must have demanded the labour of thousands of workers.

Rulers and gods

The Olmecs did not build in stone: there was little available locally. Instead, they built houses supported by wooden poles, with thatched roofs. None the less, they were among the greatest stone carvers of Mesoamerica, producing exquisite masks and figurines out of jade, obsidian and serpentine, which came from quarries in highland Mexico and Guatemala. But the Olmecs are famous above all for their giant stone heads, measuring around 2.3 m (7 ft 6 in) high and weighing 20 tonnes. Seventeen have been found so far, at San Lorenzo, La Venta and Tres Zapotes. The basalt stone used for these was quarried in the volcanic Tuxtla Mountains 70 km (42 miles) from San Lorenzo; it was probably transported by sledge, then on rafts along the rivers – an achievement only made possible with a large and well-organized labour force. These heads appear to be individual portraits, and are generally considered to represent Olmec leaders, each with his distinctive, crown-like helmet.

The leaders may also be the figures that appear in niches beneath large altar-like constructions, which probably served as thrones. They seem to be emerging from the earth, the source of all life and the place of burial, and were perhaps seen as the intermediaries between the gods and the living. Olmec deities were associated with the most powerful predatory animals of the region and ▷▷

2

The Olmecs did not have metal tools. Their giant stone heads were carved using instruments of harder stone.

Previous page:
This figure is typical of the San Agustín culture, which emerged in southern Colombia in the 1st millennium BC.

1. Another example of the tradition of robust stone sculpture of the San Agustín culture. Although now sited in an archaeological park, figures like this were originally placed in what were probably burial chambers.

1

appear in sculptures and paintings in half-human, half-animal form: as serpents, alligator-like caymans, harpy eagles, sharks and jaguars. The gods can often be identified by their cleft skulls – a feature also of the skulls of jaguars.

The Olmecs established many of the traditions of Mesoamerica that endured for the next 2000 years. Their temples consisted of raised platforms and pyramids, set around open plazas. They appear to have played a ceremonial ball game, which became better established by the Maya and Aztecs. Their mythology and pantheon of gods, inspired by

the natural world, were dominated by violent and awe-inspiring aspects of it. Figurines of men holding an inanimate child suggest that they indulged in human sacrifice, and perforating tools may have been used for ritual bloodletting – both practices that helped to reaffirm their dedicated commitment to the cosmic cycle of life.

Olmec influence spread far beyond the lowlands of the Gulf coast. It can be detected in sites in the Mexican highlands, and along the Pacific coast as far as El Salvador. In fact, the connections are so strong in some sites, such as Abaj Takalik in

2. Large numbers of small figurines, carved from jade and serpentine, were buried at La Venta as offerings to the Olmec gods.

3. A rare Chavín gold pendant has a typical theme: a cat-like animal, possibly a jaguar – an image central to the Chavín pantheon.

2

BETWEEN THE MOUNTAINS AND THE SEA

If the Olmecs were the founding culture of Mesoamerican civilization, the Chavín culture set the pattern for the Andes, where it had its greatest period of influence from about 900 to 400 BC. It takes its name from the ceremonial centre at Chavín de Huántar, in the spectacular mountain setting of the northern Andes of Peru. Chavín de Huántar consists of a complex of stone temple platforms and pyramids, with underground rooms and galleries, and over 200 sculptures of deities. The curious aspect of the Chavín pantheon (group of gods) is that it is based entirely around animals that are not found in this upland region. Most are from the tropical rainforest, such as jaguars, harpy eagles and caymans; others come from the coast, such as crabs and shellfish. Imagery of such

Guatemala, that archaeologists have suggested that the Pacific coast might have been the original Olmec heartland. But any such theories have to be based on archaeological finds alone because the Olmecs left no other records. They had no writing, only a numerical system. An even greater mystery surrounds the fate of the great cities. In about 900 BC San Lorenzo was destroyed: the monuments were systematically defaced, then buried. The same fate awaited its successor, La Venta, in 400 BC. This may have been the work of invaders – or it might equally have been some kind of ritualistic self-destruction. The Olmec civilization continued in other centres until about 250 BC.

3

animals, including imaginative hybrid forms, appears in Chavín sculpture, pottery and textiles, intertwined and rearranged in a highly distinctive style – and perhaps reflecting the use of hallucinogenic drugs taken during religious ceremonies.

Ritual and symbolism

The importance of Chavín de Huántar as a ritual centre appears to have derived from its location between mountains and the sea. Mountains were where the sun rose every day, and were the source of water for the farming communities in the valleys below. This may explain the symbolism of both the beyond-the-mountains rainforest creatures, and seashells. Furthermore, the central ritual sculpture at Chavín de Huántar is a stone shaft carved with an animal-like, fanged deity – the Lanzón, or 'smiling god' – placed in an inner chamber, between the underworld and the world of the living. The temple was perhaps seen as a kind of three-dimensional cosmic crossroads. It attracted a large following, evidence of which is the wide distribution of Chavín-influenced art and temples through much of Andean and coastal Peru. This may also indicate a new and unifying level of political control over the region. But Chavín de Huántar's role may have been overstated because this was the first site of that era to be fully studied. Temple complexes, with platforms, pyramids, plazas and stone sculpture, had developed on or nearer the coast of Peru at a much earlier date, for example at Las Haldas, from 1600 BC, or Cerro Sechín from 1200 BC. Chavín de Huántar appears to have borrowed these models.

Coastal settlements on the arid Paracas Peninsula in southern Peru emerged as another ritual centre. Hundreds of shaft tombs have been discovered, containing mummified bodies wrapped in textiles. These include pieces of intricately woven, painted and embroidered cloth, decorated with colourful, highly stylized images of animals and plants, or deities, or humans dressed in imitation of them for ritual purposes. The Paracas culture continued to flourish until about AD 400.

1

2

1. A Chavín pottery vessel. The 'stirrup spout' became a familiar format for Andean potters. Such vessels may have been used to pour libations to the gods in rituals.

2-3. Details from embroidered mummy wrappings, from Paracas. The images probably portray people who impersonated the gods in rituals, an honoured role that may have been performed by the dead person during life.

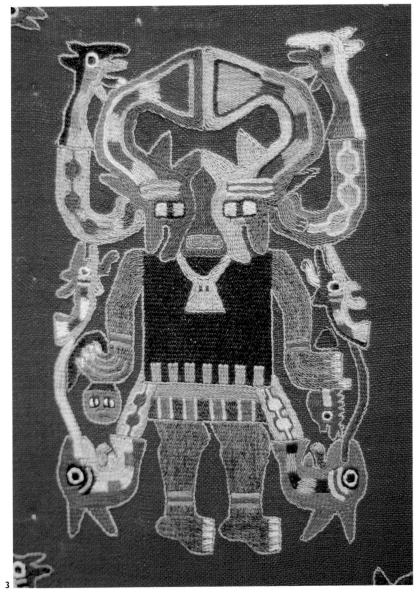

3

THE GREAT FLOURISH

THE GREAT FLOURISH

The concept of 'civilization' is closely linked to cities – and to the organization and concentration of artists and technological skills that are harnessed to create them. Political power in the world's first cities was often linked to religion and the need to secure the favour of the gods in an uncertain world. In the Americas, the first settled cultures grew up around temple sites from about 1200 BC, and these later developed into magnificent temple-cities.

The 'early classic' age of Mesoamerica, which lasted from about AD 250 to 650, coincided with a period of quite outstanding artistic flair in the Andes. The long-term political stability of the dominant regional powers – Teotihuacán, Moche and Nazca – also justifies the claim that this was a 'golden age'. But, again, history has to speak through the findings of archaeologists because written records evolved only towards the end of the period.

Previous page: The stone carvings that adorn the stairway and tiers of Teotihuacán's third largest pyramid have given rise to its name: the Temple of the Feathered Serpent (or Quetzalcoatl, as the Aztecs later called this god).

THE TRIUMPH OF THE CITY

To the Aztecs in the 14th century AD, the once-great city that lay just 40 km (25 miles) north of their capital in the highlands of central Mexico was a place of sanctity and mystery. Abandoned and left to crumble into ruins 600 years prior to their era, it already belonged to distant history. They called it Teotihuacán, 'the place of the gods'. It was long thought that the name was inspired by the sheer scale of the place – the belief that it must have been built by a race of supernatural giants. Two vast stone pyramids rise up from a broad, straight avenue (later named the Avenue of the Dead), which runs for nearly 5 km (3 miles) across the plain, surrounded by temples and residential buildings laid out on a neat, rectangular grid.

In its heyday, from about AD 200 to 650, Teotihuacán had a population estimated to be at least 125,000 and possibly 200,000. Spread over 20 sq km (8 sq miles), it was the largest city of the ancient Americas and one of the six largest cities in the world at the time. Many citizens were involved in crafts: for example, producing their distinctive pottery, or making tools and knives from obsidian (a glass-like volcanic rock), which came from mines controlled by the city. Others were traders who carried their wares across much of Mesoamerica. The presence of Teotihuacán-style buildings and pottery in distant places, such as Kaminaljuyú in Guatemala and Matacapán on the Gulf coast, indicate that the city had a widespread influence throughout the region, maintained by trade and probably reinforced by military conquest.

1. The art of Teotihuacán has an impersonal, formal flavour that contrasts with other Mesoamerican cultures. This appears to underline the city's role as a ritual centre, in the service of the gods rather than the inhabitants. The serpent image (left) was repeated hundreds of times across the four faces of the Temple of the Feathered Serpent.

Human sacrifice

Coated in white lime plaster and decorated with murals, Teotihuacán's buildings must have presented a dazzling spectacle. They were dominated by the Pyramid of the Sun, one of the world's largest pyramids, which rose to 65 m (215 ft). Beneath it lies a possible clue to the city's foundation: a cave shaped like a four-leaf clover at the end of a passageway. This was probably interpreted as an entrance to the underworld and became a shrine to the gods of creation.

The city was meticulously laid out, its slightly skewed north-south axis and street grid probably

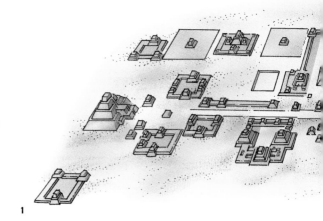

1

 THE STORM GOD

One of the main deities of Teotihuacán was the Storm God, later known by the Aztecs as Tlaloc (portrayed in a ceremonial brazier, right). He has goggle eyes and fanged teeth, and often holds a water jar in one hand and a thunderbolt in the other. The name Tlaloc means 'from the earth', and signals the vital role that this god played in bringing rain from the sky to nourish the soil. In the highlands, rituals were performed to the Storm God towards the end of the dry season, in April or May, to ensure the return of the rains. These rituals involved human sacrifice: blood, considered to be the precious vehicle of life, had to be spilled to ensure the seasonal cycle. The benefits of being favoured by the Storm God can be seen in murals in Teotihuacán, where he is pictured at the centre of earthly paradise, surrounded by dancing figures celebrating a watery landscape decked with a profusion of growth.

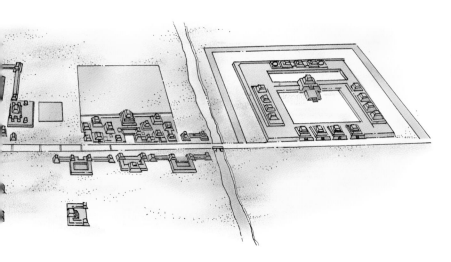

1. Teotihuacán occupied a
vast site, which included
two huge stepped pyramids
as well as the temple of
Quetzalcoatl, the Feathered
Serpent.

aligned to the setting of the sacred constellation, the Pleiades. At one end of the great ceremonial avenue is the Pyramid of the Moon, lining up with the sacred mountain Cerro Gordo, source of the water essential for the harvests needed to support a great concentration of people. Teotihuacán was not just a working city, it was a city linked to the cosmos. Rites essential to maintaining the human bond with the cosmos no doubt took place along the central avenue and on the pyramids – rows of skeletons found by the smaller Pyramid of the Feathered Serpent indicate they involved human sacrifice.

Various quarters of Teotihuacán were clearly occupied by foreign residents, identified by the distinctive styles of building and art that they brought from home. Among the foreigners were people from Veracruz, on the Gulf coast, who were the descendants of the Olmecs. They used a calendar later adopted by the entire region, and also produced some of the very first writing. This was used mainly to record events – the earliest date being AD 143. This is late, of course, compared to the first calendars, and the slow development of writing and record-keeping in the Americas is one reason why its early history is hard to pin down.

The people of Veracruz were also enthusiasts of the ball game, which was played in sloping masonry courts by men wearing leather belts and other protective equipment. The rules remain obscure, but the game is known to be connected to the creation myth, with the ball representing the sun. It was played as a ritual, in which losers were sacrificed to the gods. Teotihuacán did not have purpose-built ballcourts, but the game may have been played along the ceremonial avenue.

Another quarter of Teotihuacán was occupied by residents from Monte Albán, a city in the highlands situated 300 km (186 miles) to the south.

1

2

1. The Pyramid of the
Sun, the focal point of
Teotihuacán and one of
the largest pyramids in the
world, lies at the heart of
a vast complex of temples.

2. Among the dozen or so
structures that make up the
ritual centre of Monte
Albán is the ballcourt,
underlining the high status
accorded to the game.

Monte Albán's history stretched back to about 500 BC, and it was probably the second most important city of Mesoamerica. Set on a hilltop overlooking the Oaxaca Valley, this was the power centre of the Zapotecs, who developed a military culture that held sway over much of the outlying region. Monte Albán probably formed the first properly unified state in Mesoamerica, and seems to have retained its autonomy during the Teotihuacán era.

Early in their history, the Zapotecs had scraped the summit of Monte Albán to create a 220,000-sq m (250,000-sq yd) plaza, lined with temples and pyramids. Relief sculptures adorning one of these illustrate what Spanish observers originally took to be 'danzantes' (dancers), but they are more likely to be captive warriors, whose blood was being ritually spilled to please the gods.

1. (opposite) The so-called 'danzante' figures that decorate one of the earliest buildings of Monte Albán are believed to portray captive prisoners of war – not dancing, but writhing in pain or contorted in death.

2. The Mexican breed of hairless dog was a favourite subject of Colima potters. These dogs were bred as food, but effigies appear in burials because dogs were said to accompany the dead into the underworld.

2

Snapshots of real life

A more representative idea about daily life in Mesoamerica comes from a set of peoples living in the western highlands and on the Pacific coast, to the west of both Teotihuacán and Monte Albán. In Nayarit, Jalisco and Colima, potters brought figurine modelling to a high art. Their hollow clay figures depict warriors, farmers, animals, ball-game players, married couples and even their homes. The function of these pieces was primarily to accompany the dead: they were buried in shaft tombs dug into volcanic tufa (soft porous rock) sometime between about 300 BC and AD 300. But the sites have been widely looted and despoiled, making it hard to assess accurate dates.

Because there are no contemporary written records, we do not know what language the people of Teotihuacán spoke, nor what they called their city, or themselves.

The emergent Maya

In the highlands still farther south, in the borderlands between Mexico and Guatemala, trading centres developed at towns such as Izapa and Kaminaljuyú, at the limits of Teotihuacán's reach. The people who lived here were the Maya – a loose family of linguistically allied groups whose lands stretched from these highlands lining the Pacific coast right up to the Caribbean, through the lowland forests of Petén to the more arid Yucatán Peninsula. Like the peoples of Teotihuacán and Monte Albán, their culture centred upon pyramidal temples, but they developed their own highly distinctive art and architecture. Although the earliest manifestations of this culture occurred in the highlands, the emphasis soon shifted to the lowlands. The trading and religious centre of El Mirador, in the Petén forest, was one of their first large-scale settlements.

Teotihuacán remained the dominant city of Mesoamerica until about AD 600, and then went into decline. For reasons no one fully understands, in about AD 650 the city fell into ruin. Some of the main civic buildings were burnt down. Was this invasion, or was it revolt? Some archaeologists have argued that the city had become unsustainably large, and that the surrounding farmlands had suffered environmental damage as a result of the destruction of forests for firewood to create the large quantities of lime used in the city's plaster coating. Teotihuacán's downfall may have been caused by a conjunction of all these reasons. A similar fate befell Monte Albán shortly after this.

 EL MIRADOR

The largest pyramids built by the Maya rose to over 60 m (200 ft) above the forests of the lowland Petén region of northern Guatemala. El Mirador was perhaps the first great Maya city, flourishing from about 150 BC until AD 150. Clearly an important cult centre, the site covers about 15 sq km (6 sq miles) and includes dozens of stepped pyramids that were constructed of limestone rubble faced with red-painted lime stucco. The city probably developed as a trading centre, strategically positioned in the middle of the landmass that connects highland Mexico to the Caribbean Sea, and the Guatemala highlands to the Yucatán Peninsula. The inhabitants lived in the many settlements surrounding the ritual centre, growing maize, beans, squash and chilli, and extracting valuable products from the forests, such as pelts, feathers, hardwoods and honey. Perhaps eclipsed by the Maya cities of Tikal and Uaxactún, El Mirador declined before the age of Maya record-keeping, and its very existence was hidden beneath a thick cloak of forest until the 20th century.

ART ON A GRAND SCALE

In Peru, the influence of the Chavín had dwindled by about AD 400. Andean culture did not collapse, but political power and religious influence were now fragmented. One focus of dispersed power was the cult centre that grew up around La Tolita, in the forested Pacific coast lowlands on the border between Ecuador and Colombia. During its long flourish between 600 BC and AD 400, it produced fine metalwork, as well as highly expressive terracotta figurines. But no dominant area came to the fore until about AD 100, when a new artistic and commercial force flourished in a series of valleys running through the arid coastline in the far north of Peru.

The Moche, or Mochica, culture was named after the principal town. It clearly had a well-organized, hierarchical society, able to undertake large-scale irrigation projects that produced high-yield staples such as maize, manioc and potatoes. Its rulers and high priests were buried with gold and turquoise jewellery, beads and ornaments, as well as lavish head-dresses and cloaks. The Pyramid of the Sun in Moche, which has more than 140 million bricks, is the world's largest adobe (sun-dried brick) pyramid.

The abundance of clay was put to good use by Moche potters, who produced tens of thousands of sculptural pots. Moche skills in metalwork were equally impressive. They used every technique known in their age – hammering, embossing, repoussé work, casting, the lost-wax process – to shape and decorate copper, gold and silver into bracelets, breastplates, nosepieces and necklaces.

1. Buried in tombs, thousands of Moche stirrup vases have survived in pristine condition.

2. The tombs of Moche nobles have revealed the richness of their jewellery, such as this gold pectoral (chest ornament).

Art for the sky

Meanwhile, to the south of the Paracas Peninsula, the Nazca people farmed the coastal strip and worshipped a parallel pantheon of nature gods at adobe step pyramids. They developed equally brilliant skills in pottery, mural painting, weaving and gold work, with designs similar to those of the Paracas culture. Above all, the Nazca are famed for the giant images they traced out in the desert. By removing the oxidized surface stones to reveal the lighter coloured earth below, they created huge emblems and geometric figures, known as the 'Nazca Lines'. Some consist of long straight lines running across the desert; others are images of monkeys, birds, sharks, reptiles and other animals. They can only be fully appreciated from the sky.

The Nazca Lines have remained one of the great archaeological mysteries. The most plausible explanation refers to the central role played by rain and fertility in the Nazca religion. As in the Chavín religion, Nazca gods were associated with water – represented by exotic animals living beyond the water-giving mountains, and by sea creatures. The lines were probably used as walkways for ritual processions, directed in straight trajectories towards sacred mountains, or tracing out the shape of the gods and their emblems, which lay in full view of the chief provider of rain, the sky.

The Nazca people had influence over about 320 km (200 miles) of coast. This was maintained by warrior aggression, witnessed in one of the recurrent themes of their art: the 'trophy heads' of decapitated enemies.

MOCHE POTTERY

The form that the Moche potters almost universally adopted for their art was the stirrup-spout jar (right). Used as a container of liquids, its peculiar ringed spout also doubled as a handle. The potters mass-produced these on a grand scale, using moulds into which they pressed slabs of clay, later to be bonded, painted and fired. Subjects include deities, priests, rulers, rituals, warriors in battle, animals both mythical and real, vegetables, musicians, women giving birth, sexual acts – virtually all aspects of life. But these are not simply portrayals of reality. They are ritual vessels, needed as grave goods for burials, and each of the subjects, no matter how mundane it may seem, had sacred significance.

1. (opposite) The famous monkey figure etched into the Nazca landscape is one of several emblems featuring animals. Experiments have shown how such images could be produced from small-scale plans. The line carries on uninterrupted around the entire image – even in the elaborate spiral tail – forming a continuous path.

THE MOUND BUILDERS

In North America, the pace of development was less rapid than in Mesoamerica and the Andes. In part, this was because the rich bounty of the North American landscape permitted its inhabitants to move more slowly from foraging to agriculture. Here, societies did not generally tend towards creating towns and cities: they focused on smaller village-based societies, adapted to the economy that could be sustained from their environment. Their technology also reflected this lifestyle.

Although it produced a less spectacular legacy in artefacts and monuments, North American civilization also saw its first flourish in about 1200 BC. In the eastern woodlands in and around southern

1

1. The Serpent Mound, in southern Ohio, appears to date from the Adena period.

2

3

⭐ The Adena people of North America were exceptionally tall, averaging 2.1 m (7 ft) for a man and 1.8 m (6 ft) for a woman.

2. Death Mask Mound is one of 20 or so burial mounds at the Hopewell Culture National Historical Park near Chillicothe, Ohio.

3. Hopewell earspools and necklace, made from freshwater pearls and copper. Much of the Hopewell jewellery was made for men.

In about 100 BC, the Adena were replaced by the Hopewell people, who lived in more settled villages of pole and thatch houses. They built even larger earthworks – some more than 500 m (550 yd) across – which might contain clusters of over 20 burial mounds, as at the Hopewell Culture National Historical Park, Ohio. These burial mounds have yielded a wealth of artefacts, including jewellery and head-dresses, and cutouts of stylized animals made from turtle shell, mica, copper, silver and gold. Many of the most precious items came from sources far away, such as copper from the Great Lakes, obsidian from Yellowstone, Wyoming, alligator teeth from Florida and conch shells from the Gulf coast. Like the Adena people, the Hopewell smoked tobacco in rituals, using a form of tobacco of almost hallucinogenic strength. Their stone pipes incorporated carved and charmingly portrayed animals, such as beavers or bears. We can assume that, while these animal figures demonstrate the great observational powers of the artists, they also have cult significance.

Some unknown threat to the Hopewell people of Ohio made them convert their mounds into fortifications in about AD 500, and their mound-building days ceased. But their extensive trading network had by this time influenced a broad array of peoples right across much of the USA to the east of the Rocky Mountains. Hopewell peoples around the Great Lakes continued to build mounds in the centuries after AD 800, often in the shape of effigies, such as panthers, bears or humans. Thus the Hopewell culture effectively dominated the Midwest for about 1000 years.

Ohio, communal effort was directed towards building burial mounds and earthworks. This was the work of the Adena people, who appeared in around 700 BC, supported by their knowledge of rudimentary agriculture and their ability to establish long-distance trade links, which stretched from the Gulf of Mexico to the Great Lakes. Evidence of this trade are the grave goods buried in the log-lined tombs of the élite. Mounds, such as the Grave Creek Mound in West Virginia, rose to 20 m (65 ft) high. Earthwork enclosures took various shapes from circles to pentagons over 100 m (300 ft) in diameter, and appear to have been for ritual purposes. The most famous site is the Serpent Mound in Ohio: the earthwork that winds through the woods appears to represent a snake, which – like the Nazca Lines – can only properly be seen from the sky.

IMPERIAL ARCHITECTS

3   IMPERIAL ARCHITECTS

The history of the ancient Americas divides into three regions: North America, Mesoamerica and South America. Distinct civilizations emerged within these geographical blocks, and remained within these boundaries. By about AD 500, they had reached an age of maturity, with well-established religions, traditions, agricultural bases, trade patterns and artistic styles.

Previous page: The Toltec-Maya city of Chichén Itzá is one of the great cities of the 'post-classic' period. Toltec influences can be seen in the ranks of columns of the Temple of the Warriors, and the spartan design of the Castillo pyramid.

The political power structure at the main centres was based on a belief in the divine link between rulers and the gods. This created disciplined societies with a pyramidal hierarchy — a shape echoed in their colossal temples. But it seems the success of these complex societies carried with it the seeds of their destruction. In turn, each civilization mysteriously fell into decline and disappeared. The pattern of rule changed in the 10th century AD, when a new kind of aggressive militarism galvanized emerging nations into expansionist imperial powers.

TEMPLE CITIES OF THE MAYA

The Maya civilization developed in the Yucatán, Guatemala and west Honduras, reaching its peak after AD 300, when it dominated the region. In the Maya city of Tikal, three massive pyramids overlooked the Great Plaza. Their precipitous staircases rose towards the summit temples, which were crowned with monumental, sculpted 'roof combs'. These pyramids were not just temples, ancestral mausoleums, architectural *tours de force* – they were also a theatrical set on a grand scale. Before their brightly painted flanks, the élite of this cult city played out the lavish rituals that marked the portentous days of the Maya's complex calendar.

At the centre of proceedings were royalty, resplendent beneath animal-head crowns and plumed head-dresses. Like the gods, they appeared half-human, half-animal – an attribute also projected by the costumed deity impersonators partaking in the rituals. Among the royal retinue were warrior chiefs and high-ranking lords and ladies, all equally lavishly attired, as well as court dwarfs, and musicians who punctuated the proceedings with trumpet fanfares. Priestly scribes conducted the sacred rites in time-honoured patterns, a central part of which was sacrifice: perhaps a jaguar, or a prisoner-of-war, decapitated to please the gods. On special occasions, such as the celebration of victory or the acclamation of a

1. Temple II towers over Great Plaza at the heart of the Mayan city of Tikal, one of a pair that still bears a roof-comb crest. The tiered body of the pyramids was made of rubble, retained by stone walls that were covered in lime stucco and painted red.

1. A series of stone carvings from Yaxchilan shows the rituals marking the accession of a ruler. Here his wife, kneeling before him, performs a blood sacrifice by pulling a rope of thorns through her tongue.

2. Another series of stone carvings from the Maya city Yaxchilan records in glyphs nine generations of the city's rulers, with their accession dates up to AD 537. The stones were probably mounted on a building by a later ruler in the 8th century AD to reinforce his ancestral claim.

1

2

new dynastic heir, the royal family would spill their own blood: a king would pierce his penis with a stingray spine; his wife would pass a rope sewn with thorns through her tongue.

A written record

Such scenarios are not entirely conjecture. The Maya have left more information about their lives than any preceding American culture – in mural paintings, decorated pottery, relief sculptures and hieroglyphic writing. A combination of picture-writing and phonetics, Maya glyphs appear on stone sculptures, on the lintels and stairways of temples, and on steles (stone pillars) erected as monuments. Writing was also used in the many long, folded books, called codices (singular: codex), which the Maya made from sheets of dried animal skin or maguey (agave) leaves.

Only a handful of these codices have survived, all from the late Maya periods. Their historical information is dated to the day. Through astro-nomical observation, the Maya developed one of the most precise calendars of any ancient civil-ization. The calendar, called the 52-year Calendar Round, operated on two systems simultaneously: 20 named days rotating 13 times in a 260-day year; and a parallel year of 365 days. These meshed to provide a different name for every day in each 52-year cycle. They also used a Long Count system, which traced time back to a starting point thought to be the equivalent of 13 August 3114 BC.

The Maya texts deal with the affairs of the ruling élite: the details of ritual observance, divination, mythology and astronomy. Scribes were probably part of this élite, and they guarded their status jealously. Not much is known about the rest of the population, most of whom clearly lived in adobe-and-thatch huts in suburbs and villages around ceremonial city centres. Some were traders, or artisans who produced the rich array of Maya crafts – pottery, jade sculptures, textiles, jewellery and decorative featherwork. But most people farmed gardens and fields for maize, beans, squash, manioc and cotton, and kept them watered with intricate irrigation systems. Many would also, no doubt, have had to give up some of their time to the huge task of building the pyramids – all achieved without metal tools or wheeled vehicles. Quite how this work was organized remains unknown.

City-states

By AD 600, in the 'Late Classic' era of the Maya civilization, the forested lowlands of eastern Mexico, northern Guatemala and Belize, and the more arid Yucatán Peninsula to the north, were dotted with dozens of cities, each with its own elaborate temple complex of pyramids, platforms, plazas and palaces. Typically, the pyramids were built over the tombs of the ruling élite.

Tikal (population 80,000) was exceptionally large. Other cities – Uxmal and Chichén in the north, Palenque and Yaxchilán in the heartlands, and Copán in the south, in western Honduras – probably had around 20,000 inhabitants. They appear to have operated as city-states, each ruled by

 CHOCOLATE

The peoples of ancient Mesoamerica had a passion for chocolate, but it was a very different product from the sugar-laden sweet of today. The Aztec term Xocolatl (from which our word chocolate is derived) meant 'sour water'. The essential ingredient was cacao (a Maya word), the seeds or 'beans' of the cacao tree, which grew in the tropical forests of Central and South America. Harvested and dried, the beans were traded across Mesoamerica as a precious commodity (shown in a codex, right). To prepare them for consumption, they were roasted, ground into powder and mixed with water to produce a thick, frothy, bitter drink. This was one of the great luxuries of Maya life: it played a role in the Maya vision of heaven, and had a special place in sacred rituals.

1. The Cotzumalhuapa culture developed in a cocoa-growing region on the Pacific plain of Guatemala after the 6th century. Although apparently independent of the Mayas and Teotihuacán, it was clearly influenced by both. A series of stone steles depicts ball players, here promising an offering to their god.

hereditary chiefs, perhaps with power over smaller vassal cities. They were also constantly jockeying for influence, power-broking through dynastic marriages, or at war. The sacred ball game may well have played a part in resolving disputes.

The Maya did not extend their territory outside the Maya homelands, but they had a wide cultural impact, largely through trade. They had close trading relationships with the key outlying urban centres, such as El Tajín, the main focus of the classic Veracruz culture that emerged in old Olmec territory, and a centre of cocoa production. A few Maya satellite towns also developed in the highlands of Mexico, such as Cacaxtla and Xochicalco to the south of Teotihuacán, although these were the exception rather than the rule.

After the fall of Teotihuacán in about AD 650, the Maya were left as the main regional power. But once again the familiar Mesoamerican dénouement was about to unfold: another superb civilization inexplicably collapsed. One by one, the Maya cities were abandoned. The date remains vague: the sculptors who had trumpeted the achievements of the leaders in stone glyphs suddenly fell silent – half way through the job, on 10 February AD 822, in the case of one inscription in Copán. No one would have funded the reporting of bad news, so we are left to guess at the cause. Warfare may have been responsible, or perhaps the land became degraded by forest clearing. Perhaps the Maya simply stopped believing in the religious orthodoxy that dominated their lives. By AD 900, almost all the great Maya cities had been abandoned to the invasive forest or scrub and the corrosive climate of the arid Yucatán.

1. A frieze on the Nunnery at Uxmal. A distinctive style of Maya architecture developed in the Puuc region of the Yucatán, marked by its elaborate, mosaic-like stonework façades.

2. The 'frontal god' appears in the middle of the Gate of the Sun at Tiahuanaco, carved in low relief on a stone lintel weighing 9 tonnes.

THE BONAMPAK PAINTINGS

Maya art is often held to be more representational and expressive than that of other Mesoamerican and South American cultures. This is sometimes fiercely disputed, but the extraordinary late 8th-century murals of Bonampak, a ruined Maya city in eastern Chiapas, Mexico, near Yaxchilán, provide a case in point. They represent the main events in the life of the last ruler, Chaan Muan: a modern copy (right) shows him leading a military raid to win prisoners for sacrifice. Many elements of traditional stylization are present, such as the use of profile faces and the presentation of symbolic regalia, but these images have a dynamic flare that sets them apart. Despite the bloodthirsty subject matter, the figures are painted with expressive freedom, tinged with humour and humanity.

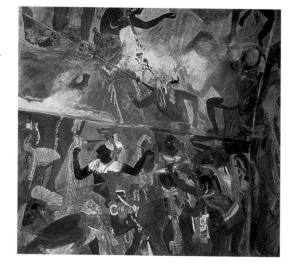

EMPIRES OF THE ANDES

After the long dominance of the coastal cultures in western South America, in about AD 400 the focus shifted to the High Andes. At 3000 m (10,000 ft) above sea level, the city of Tiahuanaco (also spelled Tiwanaku) was the highest city of the ancient Americas. Perhaps dating back to 1500 BC, it stood on the shores of Lake Titicaca (which has since retreated) and on the edge of the Altiplano. This treeless plain is also the biggest area of level ground in the Andes: with careful irrigation it could be coaxed into producing crops, notably potatoes, and grazing for llamas and alpacas.

At the edge of the lake stood an extensive temple complex, which is now an austere ruin of open plazas, stone walls, gateways, a 15-m (50-ft) high pyramid-like platform and ranks of columns. The stone, all worked by stone tools, is neatly finished, but massive: some of the pyramid blocks weigh 100 tonnes. These could only have reached the site by raft. Large monolithic sculptures of the gods, up to 7.6 m (25 ft) tall and carved in low relief, dot the site. An image of the main Tiahuanaco deity appears on a massive single block of stone known as the Gate of the Sun: this is the stiff 'frontal god', with its mask-like face. Another common deity is pictured in profile, with wings. Tiahuanaco was

2

clearly a religious and political centre, but it was also the source of distinctive pottery, goldwork with turquoise inlay, and textiles decorated with geometric patterns. Signs of its influence in the highlands are found in the wide distribution of Tiahuanaco-style artefacts that have been recovered as far south as northern Chile and Argentina.

Military power

The same gods appear in the Huari (or Wari) culture, named after a city 700 km (435 miles) northwest of Tiahuanaco. After AD 600, Huari's influence spread north, as witnessed in a series of buildings in major towns and along the trade routes. These appear to be garrisons and administration centres, for the people of Huari acquired territory by military

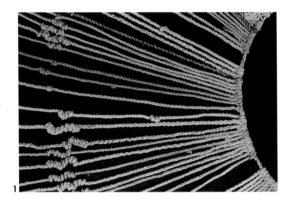

conquest. They created an empire that stretched some 1000 km (620 miles) along the Andes and the coast. The Huari culture left scant record of their exploits: unlike the Maya, they did not have writing. But they did have the use of the quipu – tassel-like cords with which information could be recorded by colour-coding and knots.

The Huari and Tiahuanaco empires appear to have kept separate spheres of influence, but shared power over a swathe of central territory between the highlands and the coast. The Huari culture faded in about AD 800, as the result of some unspecified crisis, and the townships fragmented into warring factions. Pachacamac, the ceremonial centre on the coast, emerged as a minor regional power in central Peru. Tiahuanaco ruled the south of Peru for another 300 years. It was more than 400 years after the fall of the Huari that the Incas arose from Cuzco, in the heart of former Huari territory. But the Huari legacy of military expansionism provided a model that had a critical bearing on the subsequent history of South America.

> ⭐ In Mesoamerica, the wheel was not used for transport or for making pottery, but it was not completely unknown. Toy-like clay models of animals with four wheels at their feet have been found.

CITIES OF THE NORTH

Although poorly documented, there was clearly contact between the prominent civilizations across the American continents through trade. It is hard to measure the impact of these links, but they may well have been the cause of radical change in the eastern woodlands of North America.

After about AD 800, the Hopewell cultures of the eastern woodlands were eclipsed by a new wave of agriculturists. They occupied the flood valleys of the central reaches of the Mississippi and its many tributaries, harvesting a new, fast-growing strain of maize as well as beans, both of which appear to have originated in Mexico. The 'three sisters' – maize, beans and squash – increased the available food resources, which enabled far higher concentrations of population and the emergence of a new type of culture called 'Mississippian' (the term applies to widely dispersed cultures across the southern states).

The Mississippian settlement of Cahokia, in East St Louis, Illinois, was the first real city of North America. By 1050, it had a population of perhaps 30,000 and covered 13 sq km (5 sq miles). At the centre was a massive earthwork temple mound (called Monk's Mound), measuring 316 m (1036 ft) long, 241 m (790 ft) wide and 30 m (100 ft) high – perhaps also the product of contacts with Mesoamerica. The rich grave goods and human sacrifices found in the hundred or so burial mounds show the city was ruled by a hierarchical élite, who probably earned their position by prowess in war, for territorial possession now

2

1. In a quipu, messages and records could be stored and encoded in the colours and lengths of the cords, and in the style and position of the knots.

2. Clay figurine of a water carrier. The very limited distribution of the Pacha-camac style indicates a cult centre rather than a military power.

1

became an essential element of power. With their improved food supplies, populations were rising fast, so the Mississippians needed to control and colonize increasing areas of the fertile flood plains, which they defended with stockaded villages. Instead of ploughing, they depended on the annual deposit of silt to refresh their fields, which they worked with flint-tipped hoes. And instead of creating new fields by woodland clearance and irrigation, they expanded up the river valleys and fought over existing areas of productive land. It was at about this time that the bow and arrow, introduced in North America in about AD 500, began to take over from the spear-thrower as the prime weapon of the North Americans.

Cliff-dwellers

Mesoamerica also had an impact on developments in the southwest of North America. Today, the region is divided by the border between Mexico and the USA. In Mesoamerica, trade routes clearly extended through the whole region.

Whatever the influence of Mesoamerica, the result was an utterly different culture to that of the Mississippians. By about AD 600 there were three maize-growing cultures in the arid lands to the northeast of the Gulf of California, around the Colorado River and the Rio Grande.

The Hohokam, who inhabited this region, were experts in irrigation farming, extending the areas of useful land with ingenious systems of dams, canals and sluice gates. Their communities included platform mounds and ballcourts, which has led to the suggestion that they were descendants of migrants from Mexico.

The Mogollon, from the Mimbres area of southwest New Mexico, were farmers and foragers. They are famous for their distinctive pottery , which has striking stylized motifs of animals or humans painted in two colours (usually black on white). Most of the surviving examples have been punctured with holes because the Mogollon placed them over the heads of the dead – but first they would 'kill' the pot with a hole.

The third group are called the Anasazi, although this is a pejorative word (meaning something like 'old enemies') used by the Navajo, a native American Indian people who occupied the region after the 15th century. The term Anasazi applies to a culture that spans well over 1000 years, from the Basket Makers dating back to at least 100 BC, to the Pueblo peoples of the 13th century AD. It centred on the 'Four Corners', where Arizona, New Mexico, Utah and Colorado meet. By about AD 900, the Anasazi had developed a distinctive form of communal housing that combined their traditional circular pit houses with multi-storeyed, flat-roofed rectangular dwellings made from adobe or stone.

1. The centre of Cahokia was protected by a stockade, while the river provided a major transport artery. The focal pyramid, Monk's Mound, has a larger base than that of the Great Pyramid in Egypt.

2. Pueblo pot depicting deer. Hunting remained an important source of food in the southwest: the red lines indicate the heart, to guide the hunters' arrows.

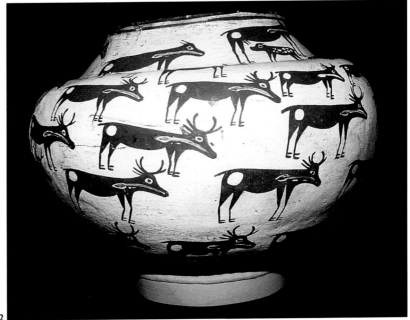

2

These clusters were often built to form a shape such as a D, O or L. The Spanish later called such a settlement a pueblo, and this became the name for the culture as a whole in its later form.

Agriculture was the main occupation of the Pueblo peoples. They farmed the river valleys, raising maize, pumpkins, beans, cotton and turkeys. They also produced pottery and textiles, and traded in turquoise and shells from the Pacific coast. Religion played a key role in their lives. The circular pit houses evolved into ritual centres and male clubhouses, called kivas. Entered by a ladder through a hole in the roof, they symbolized the sacred underworld of the ancestor spirits. Some of the Pueblo peoples were cliff-dwellers, living at first in villages perched on the crests of sheer canyons, and later on shelves in the canyon walls. Many of these settlements, notably at Mesa Verde in Colorado, and at the Canyon de Chelly in Arizona, display a remarkable bond with the grandeur of the landscape.

The most impressive concentration of Pueblo towns is in Chaco Canyon, in New Mexico, where 70 settlements centred on the largest of them all, Pueblo Bonito. This culture suddenly faded from existence in the late 13th century. A drought lasting from 1276 to 1299 may have proved the last straw, but there may have been other contributory causes, such as invasion, or the degradation of land through deforestation.

1. (opposite) The ruins of the 'White House' in the Canyon de Chelly, Arizona. Set in a niche well above the valley floor, its 80 rooms could house an entire village.

2. Cliff-dwellings at Pueblo Puye, Santa Clara, New Mexico. Pueblo buildings were constructed of roughly hewn stone blocks, adobe and timber.

2

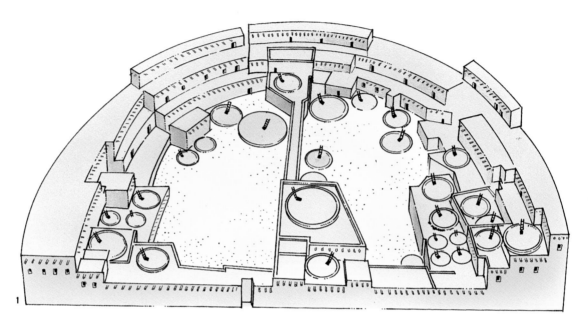

1

 PUEBLO BONITO

Pueblo Bonito means 'pretty village' – a name that distinctly undersells this haunting ruin in Chaco Canyon, northern New Mexico. Built in phases from about AD 900 to 1100, this neatly defined D-shaped structure once contained about 650 rooms and housed perhaps 1200 people. In fact, it was the biggest apartment block in the USA until the 19th century. The walls were of quarried sandstone, faced with adobe mud, and the thousands of wooden beams were imported from forests 100 km (60 miles) away. The village was entered by ladders, which could be drawn up over the defensive walls. Within lay a plaza dotted with the entry holes to the underground ceremonial kivas. Tiers of dwellings rising to five storeys lined the curved back of the settlement. The flat roofs served as balconies, grain-drying surfaces and outdoor living areas. Pueblo Bonito was abandoned in the late 13th century, probably as a result of drought and persistent crop failure.

1. The dwellings at Pueblo Bonito were arranged around the D-shaped perimeter. Thirty-seven circular kivas (clubhouses) of various sizes are distributed across the site, some within the dwellings.

2. (opposite) Pueblo Bonito lies on the eastern side of Chaco Canyon. Roads radiate out from it, connecting the 12 pueblos in the canyon.

TOLTEC WARRIORS

Back in the legendary past, nomadic warriors of the Chichimeca people, from somewhere in or beyond the far north of Mesoamerica, descended into central Mexico.

They installed themselves on an arid plain to the north of the Valley of Mexico and merged with the sedentary locals to create the new military power of the region, the Toltecs, named after their capital city Tollán, better known as Tula. Their culture owed much to Teotihuacán. This is reflected in their stark and formal sculpture, but the Toltecs also produced some fine metalwork and uniquely expressive pottery figurines of warriors. After about AD 950, by waging expansionist wars, the Toltecs gained control of a large empire and their influence spread as far south as the Maya lands. They took with them their cult following of Quetzalcoatl (the Feathered Serpent), a god linked with the planet Venus and closely associated with the ruling dynasty.

Toltec-Maya

Tula developed into a splendid city, with a palace, pyramidal temples, two ballcourts and rows of columns that supported timber-beamed roofs. In about 1200 the city was destroyed, perhaps by a further wave of Chichimeca invaders. Legend has another way of accounting for Tula's demise: Their god Quetzalcoatl was driven out by the rival

1. One of the principal pyramids of Tula is surmounted by carved columns that once supported the roof, while a covered colonnade surrounded the courtyard below.

2. A statue of the Maya god Chac Mool gazes out nonchalantly over Chichén Itzá from the upper level of the Temple of the Warriors.

deity Tezcatlipoca, god of the night sky, and a group of Toltecs, loyal followers of Quetzalcoatl, fled to the Yucatán Peninsula. In reality, it seems that the Toltecs exploited political turmoil between the two largest Yucatán cities of the 'post-classic' Maya age, Mayapán and Chichén. This was where their allies, the Itzá people from the Mexican coastal lowlands of Tabasco, had come to live after the collapse of the Maya cities. Chichén Itzá, as it became known, now enjoyed a Toltec-Maya renaissance.

The northern Yucatán receives very little rainfall. The inhabitants of Chichén Itzá were dependent on natural sink-hole wells beneath the limestone crust. These vital lifelines were held to be sacred, and they were the focus of elaborate rituals. The story that women and captive warriors were thrown into the wells as a sacrifice was thought to be a legend, until archaeological dives in 1905 yielded a large number of skeletons of women, as well as a number of men and children.

After the fall of the Toltecs, a new military power – the Mixtecs – emerged in the central highlands. From about 1200, the Mixtecs extended their control across Zapotec country in the Oaxaca valley, and rehabilitated the deserted Zapotec capital Monte Albán (▷ p.31). The Mixtecs were famed for producing some of the best gold and silverware in Mesoamerica. Metallurgy had become established in Mesoamerica only a few centuries earlier, and the Mixtecs were the masters of this art. Their skills placed them in a position of high respect when the next military power arose in Mesoamerica in the 14th century – the Aztecs.

2

The Pyramid of Quetzalcoatl in Cholula is the largest pyramid in the world. It has a total volume of 3.3 million cu m (116.5 million cu ft); the largest pyramid in Egypt occupies 2.4 million cu m (84.8 million cu ft).

AZTECS AND INCAS

4 AZTECS AND INCAS

Two civilizations emerged in the 14th and 15th centuries to dominate Mesoamerica and the Andes in parallel. There was little contact between them, but they shared many common features. Both cultures were aggressive empire builders; both capitalized on the long legacy of civilization in their spheres of influence to create power-centres of unprecedented splendour; and both inflicted a heavy burden of obligations within their empires, creating a groundswell of resentment that left them vulnerable when a new and devastating threat arrived from outside.

Above all, what the Aztec and Inca civilizations share is a legacy of history. Neither was longlived: the Aztec empire lasted no more than 200 years, the Inca empire less than 100 years. Yet we know more about them than about any preceding American civilization because they were both observed, wondered at – and then unceremoniously wrecked by European invaders.

Previous page: Set high in the Andes, the Inca city of Machu Picchu is one of the most exhilarating of all American archaeological sites. Abandoned in the 16th century, it was rediscovered only in 1911.

EMPIRE OF THE SUN

At the heart of the central highlands of Mexico lies the Valley of Mexico, the floor of which was once filled by a large, snaking lake called Lake Texcoco. In the turmoil after the fall of the Toltecs in Tula (▷ pp.58–9), a number of tribes came into the valley and occupied the shores of the lake. A latecomer was a Nahuatl-speaking nomadic group from the north called the Mexicas, or Aztecs, who – according to their own legends – had wandered for 200 years before settling in the valley. In about 1325, they founded a city on a swampy island in the middle of the lake, and named it Tenochtitlán.

A century later the Aztecs were powerful enough to enter a military triple alliance with the neighbouring cities of Texcoco and Tlacopan, and they set about conquering first their neighbours, then acquiring an ever-greater empire across the breadth of Mesoamerica. By 1480, the Aztecs had become the dominant partners in the alliance; Tenochtitlán was now effectively the capital of an empire that controlled 38 provinces and stretched from the Atlantic to the Pacific, and as far south as the old Maya lands (▷ p.47).

The Aztecs won their empire by ruthless military aggression, and maintained it by posting military garrisons in the occupied lands. These

CULTURES OF MESOAMERICA

Tula
Lake Texcoco
Valley of Mexico
Teotihuacán
Tenochtitlán
Veracruz
Teotitlan
Gulf of Mexico
San Lorenzo
Monte Albán
Oaxaca Valley
PACIFIC OCEAN

homeland of Tlaxcalans

1. By the late 15th century, the Aztecs, with their capital at Tenochtitlán, had become the dominant power in Mesoamerica.

garrisons also enforced the annual payment of tribute – a massive quantity of goods, which the Aztecs demanded of their subject nations. Tenochtitlán became wealthy, the hub of trade, and a vibrant centre for arts that mirrored all the preceding traditions of the Mesoamerican civilizations.

Class system

Aztec society was strictly hierarchical, led from the top by its semi-divine ruler, the tlatoani (literally, 'speaker'). He was elected from the family of the ruling dynasty by an educated and privileged élite of nobles, who also acted as his advisers and chief administrators. Among them was his all-important deputy, curiously called the cihuacoatl ('snake woman'), although the position was always held by a man. The cihuacoatl was in charge of running the government, the courts and the civil service. Military chiefs also played a key role in govern-ment. They belonged to two orders of privileged knights, the Eagles and the Jaguars – a concept borrowed from the Toltecs. Access to the highest ranks of the military was won by bravery on the battlefield, and judged by the number of captives personally taken. The sons of nobles had access to schools, where they learnt law, history, astronomy, mathematics, religious observance, combat and the rudiments of pictographic writing (otherwise the preserve of priestly scribes). Priests, who were also ranked among the nobility, were trained in seminary schools. They led a life apart and remained celibate. Among their important tasks was the observation

1

1. Excavations at the Great Pyramid (Templo Mayor) of Tenochtitlán, starting in 1978, have revealed a large number of statues and other artefacts, as well as the foundations of at least four earlier pyramids.

2. The Calendar Stone was kept in Tenochtitlán's main square. Carved as a disk 3.6 m (11 ft 9 in) in diameter, it represents the Aztecs' concept of the history of the world, and its destruction, in five phases.

2

of the calendar: based on the Maya model, it marked the sacred significance of the passage of time and dictated all activities, from the agricultural seasons to celebrations for the cycles of the cosmos.

Below the élite was a broad band of freemen and commoners, who had rights to land for farming and building. These included artisans who produced the full range of Mesoamerican crafts. Among the active and prosperous community of traders were the secretive pochteca, merchants belonging to a guild that controlled the long-distance trade in luxury goods. The Aztecs did not use beasts of burden or wheeled vehicles, so porters played an important part in this trade. They covered more than 50 km (30 miles) a day, carrying on their backs loads of up to 45 kg (100 lb).

 AZTEC TRIBUTE LISTS

The penalty for defeat at war by the Aztecs, and the price of coming under the protection of their empire, was the payment of annual tribute. Long lists of tribute demanded were drawn up by scribes in Tenochtitlán, with each of the items illustrated next to the quantities required (right). They usually consisted of basic agricultural produce and raw materials, plus manufactured goods. One province, for example, was instructed to supply 123,400 cotton cloaks, 8000 cu m (10,500 cu yd) of maize, and similarly large quantities of beans, chillies, cocoa beans, salt and incense. Demands for tribute were delivered by much-feared and loathed collectors, and non-payment was punished with raids and additional tribute demands, as well as prisoners for sacrifice.

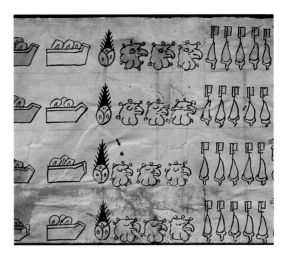

The mass of people lived by farming and market trading. All ordinary Aztecs were members of clan-like groupings called calpulli, which owned land and had their own temples, social structures, schools and festivals. Aztec citizens led ordered lives; crime was minimal, and punishments were strictly regulated by law. Health was maintained by a sophisticated knowledge of herbal cures, a plentiful diet and also a high level of cleanliness. Almost all houses were equipped with steam rooms for bathing. On the lowest rung of society were the slaves. By and large, they were treated well, and could earn their freedom. All members of society displayed their rank with their hairstyles, clothing and jewellery. Only nobles, for example, could wear shoes, or an ornament through their pierced lower lip.

Living on the lake

Tenochtitlán depended on an ingenious system of farming that took place in the shallows of Lake Texcoco. A network of fertile garden plots, accessed by the narrow canals that separated them, was created by piling up earth and mud and anchoring it with mats, wooden stakes and tree roots. Heavily fertilized with manure, these 'chinampas' produced large quantities of vegetables and fruit, as well as flowers, which were used for house decorations and gifts. There were chinampas around the island of Tenochtitlán, but most were in the southern arm of the lake, around Xochimilco ('place of the fields of flowers'), where some still survive today, along with the last remnants of Lake Texcoco.

1. Harvesting maize, an illustration from a 16th-century Florentine codex. The standard dress for men was a simple loin cloth, worn with a cloak at ceremonies.

2. The waterways and chinampas gardens of Xochimilco, to the south of Mexico City, still bear witness to the intense agricultural fertility that supported Tenochtitlán.

This southern part of the lake, and Tenochtitlán itself, benefited from fresh water as a consequence of an ingenious dyke that divided the lake in two. Rivers flowed into Lake Texcoco, but not out of it: moisture evaporated, but left behind an accumulation of minerals, gradually turning the remaining water salty. Water in the southern part of the lake was fresher because of a greater run-off from surrounding hills and mountains. The dyke separated the salty water of the northern reaches from the fresher water of the south. It was named after its builder, Netzahualcóyotl, king of Texcoco (reigned 1431–72), who was also famed as a poet and

☆ According to some estimates, when the Great Temple of Tenochtitlán was inaugurated in 1487, some 80,000 people were sacrificed to the Aztec gods.

2

lawmaker and did much to underpin Texcoco's status as an intellectual and cultural centre, even after Tenochtitlán had risen to dominance.

Blood imperatives

The Aztecs were constantly at war in pursuit not only of tribute, but also of prisoners. Most ancient American cultures practised human sacrifice, but the Aztecs took the practice to extremes. Their chief tribal god was Huitzilopochtli, the sun god, and they believed that constant offerings of blood – especially that of courageous captives – were essential to persuade him to return each day at dawn. Some 10,000 people a year were killed on the summits of the pyramid temples. Held down with their backs over the sacrificial stone, their hearts were cut out by priests wielding obsidian knives. The majority of victims were prisoners of war.

On major occasions, such as the dedication of a new temple, hundreds of victims were sacrificed in a day, so that the temple steps were awash with blood. Their skulls were then proudly displayed on a skull-rack, or tzompantli. The temples reeked of death and priests were covered in gore. To honour the god of springtime, Xipe Totec, victims were flayed (skinned) alive, and the priests then dressed in their skins. Statues of Xipe Totec were likewise dressed in the flayed skins of sacrificial victims. Other important gods demanded similar devotions. They included the mother goddess Coatlicue ('serpent skirt'), as well as the Toltec deities Tlaloc, the rain god; Quetzalcoatl, the Feathered Serpent; and Quetzalcoatl's great rival, Tezcatlipoca.

1

2

1. The goddess Coatlicue ('serpent skirt'), mother of Huitzilopochtli, was both a creator and destroyer of life.

2. A human skull, decorated with stripes of turquoise and lignite, forms an image of the god Tezcatlipoca, dark rival to Quetzalcoatl.

A few peoples within the Aztec empire, such as the independently minded Tlaxcalans to the east of the Valley of Mexico, resisted conquest, so did not pay tribute. As a compromise, they fought ritualized battles called the Xochiyaoyotl, or Flowery Wars (flower petals were a metaphor for fallen warriors). Contestants from both sides dressed in their finery of pelts, feathers, animal headdresses, regalia and war trophies, and faced each other at a chosen site on an auspicious day. The aim of this massive gladiatorial combat was to win as many captives as possible, preferably unharmed – although this was not easy, as the warriors were armed with lances, axes and clubs spiked with razor-sharp obsidian. Captives from these ritual battles were particularly highly prized. They were treated with respect, and then sacrificed. They may have gone to their deaths willingly, proud to offer themselves to the gods, and thus gain access to paradise with honour.

The Flowery Wars exemplify the extraordinary tension that ran through the Aztec world. The Aztecs were highly disciplined, orderly and pious. They respected humility, obedience and hard work. These virtues created a society of great cohesion and sophistication, while at the same time yoking all participants to an unceasing cycle of religious imperatives of extreme destructive violence.

 TENOCHTITLÁN

Tenochtitlán was founded according to an ancient Aztec prophecy, which spoke of a great city rising from the place where an eagle was seen devouring a serpent while sitting on a cactus growing out of a rock. Such a place was identified on an island in Lake Texcoco, but the Aztecs had to overcome huge logistical difficulties to build there, on an unpromising mixture of swamp and reclaimed land. All materials had to be brought across the lake on rafts, including large quantities of quarried stone and the massive tree-trunks that were driven into the mud as piles to hold the foundations. The result was a dazzling city (right), criss-crossed by canals and linked to the mainland by causeways. By 1500, Tenochtitlán had some 200,000 inhabitants and was much larger than any other city at that time. Almost all of Tenochtitlan has now been obliterated by Mexico City, which stands on its site.

CONQUERING THE ANDES

After the collapse of the Huari empire in about AD 800 (▷ p.50), the High Andes returned to another period of power struggles. But during the 13th century, a new empire emerged in the north, from the coastal city of Chan Chan, close to where the Moche (▷ pp.35-6) had flourished some 800 years earlier. The Chimú people conquered the Moche and Chavín lands, and spread north as far as the modern border with Ecuador. In addition to military prowess, they showed engineering skills, using complex irrigation schemes to turn the arid valleys into fertile farmlands. They even built an 80-km (50-mile) long canal to bring water to Chan Chan from the neighbouring Chicama river.

Chan Chan is a now a vast adobe ruin. Covering 15 sq km (6 sq miles), it was the largest town of ancient South America, and may have had a population of 50,000. There are nine large compounds: excavations suggest that these were the successive palaces of the god-kings. It appears that when a king died he was buried in his palace, along with his sacrificed wives and grave goods, and then the palace became a temple.

The Chimú empire lasted for about a century until 1472, when it was conquered by the Incas. Chimú craftworkers had preserved the artistic inheritance of the Moche in gold and silverwork, textiles, and a distinctive form of black ceramics in Moche style. These skills were recognized by the Incas, who looted the wealth of Chan Chan and sent the best craft-workers to their capital, Cuzco, 1000 km (600 miles) to the south.

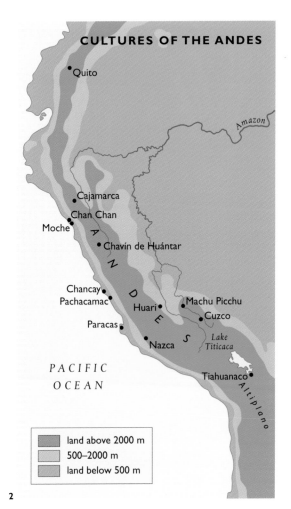

CULTURES OF THE ANDES

land above 2000 m
500–2000 m
land below 500 m

2

1. (opposite) The interior walls of some of Chan Chan's royal compounds are composed of distinctive lattice-like open diamonds of adobe brick.

2. The Chimú empire, with its capital at coastal Chan Chan, was absorbed in the 1470s by the empire of the Inca, whose capital was highland Cuzco.

1

The Incas

The Incas dated their occupation of the highland city of Cuzco to the reign of a semi-legendary 13th-century king called Manco Capac, said to have descended from the sun god. He was the first 'inca' – the title given to the dynastic god-kings. We know the empire and people by this name, but they called their land Tahuantinsuyu, 'land of four quarters', for their empire was divided into four regions.

The Incas won their empire through military conquest, modelling their strategy on the successes of Huari and Chimú. Formerly local warlords in Cuzco, they began their expansion under a series of great Incas, starting with Pachacuti Inca Yupanqui (reigned 1438–71). By the reign of his grandson Huayna Capac (1493–1525), their empire covered the entire Andes and the coast from Ecuador to central Chile. It was by far the largest empire of the ancient Americas. They also ran a more efficient, centrally organized government than any other

 COCA

Many of the figurines produced by Andean potters show one cheek bulging with coca leaves. The leaves of the coca shrub contain cocaine. Chewed in a wad (or 'quid'), they provide a fairly mild narcotic effect. Like everything in the Inca world, coca had a sacred significance, and formed part of rituals. It was also used as an anaesthetic and an aid to endurance. Powdered lime, usually made from seashells, was added to the quid to assist the extraction of cocaine from the leaves. Coca-chewers dipped a stick into a small flask containing the lime and then licked the stick. A coca-chewer's full kit consisted of a pouch for the coca leaves, and the powder flask with a dipper stick. These are often found among grave goods.

nation in the region. In 1471 Topa Inca Yupanqui (reigned 1471–93) imposed the Inca language Quechua as the common tongue to be used across the empire.

The empire prospered by producing prodigious quantities of food, in particular maize and potatoes, from irrigated valleys and the extensive terraces that rose up the steep hillsides surrounding the villages. The past extent of these is still evident today, across the Andes. Farmers also raised llamas as beasts of burden, alpacas for wool, and dogs, guinea pigs and ducks for meat.

By and large, the various peoples collaborated willingly with the Inca system, bound to the central government not only by its bureaucracy and the economic structure, but also by religious beliefs.

Sun god

To the Incas, their ruler was a god-king, the son of the sun, and Cuzco was a cosmic centre; its name meant 'navel' (of the world). Cuzco was in fact a ceremonial centre that was reserved for the élite only. Richly painted and decorated in gold and colourful hanging textiles, it was an orderly city of palaces and temples. The central focus of the city was the Temple of the Sun, which was the setting for the annual Festival of the Sun, at which the dressed, mummified bodies of former Inca rulers were exhibited for worship.

The ordinary people of Cuzco lived in the 12 surrounding satellite towns. They were not permitted to look the Inca in the face, and even ▷▷

1. These ceremonial gloves of beaten gold formed part of a Chimú burial. The Incas appropriated the skills of craftsmen from the cultures that fell under their control.

2. A 16th-century engraving by Theodor de Bry gives a Europeanized view of how Cuzco looked at the height of the Inca empire.

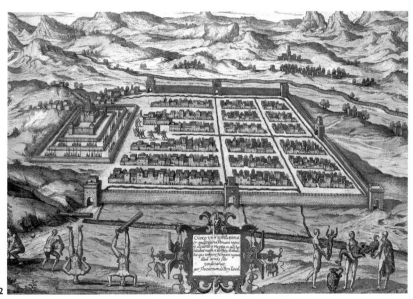

2

nobles – all relatives of the ruler – would put on workmen's baskets and grovel before him to demonstrate their lowly status. The Inca married his sister as his principal wife, but also had hundreds of other wives and concubines, and as many children. Many of these women were expected to accompany the Inca on his journey to paradise after death, and were strangled for burial alongside him. The new Inca was chosen from among the many sons, creating a regular round of dynastic squabbles.

The Incas revered the ruined city of Tiahuanaco as the source of their religion. The supreme deity was Viracocha, the creator god and ruler of all living things, who had visited the kingdom in legendary times, then headed off across the Pacific Ocean where the sun set – perhaps one day to return and create a new golden age.

Empire building

The Inca empire encompassed all the areas of earlier Andean civilizations. The extraordinarily rich range of craftwork that this territory produced became part of the Inca culture, and there was a vigorous trade in pottery, textiles and goldwork that spanned all four quarters of the Inca lands.

The Inca contributed an extraordinary skill in architecture. Masons shaped large rocks into polygonal, smooth blocks, which fitted neatly together without mortar. Here again, most of the stonework was achieved with stone tools, although bronze was used to make chisels and crowbars. The jigsaw-like features of the massive stone walls is a distinctive mark of Inca building, which has proved well adapted to this earthquake-prone landscape.

Previous page: Extensive terracing gave Machu Picchu the agricultural land it needed to survive in its precipitous setting. The mountaintop location of this city begins to make sense in the context of the Inca religion, which connected mountains with the constellations and cosmos.

 INCA CHILD SACRIFICE

In recent years some remarkable archaeological remains have been found on remote peaks of the Andes, in Peru, Chile and Argentina. They are the fully dressed bodies of children, preserved from decay by freezing temperatures. There used to be thousands of such graves (such as the mountaintop tombs in Colombia, right) in the Inca lands, in almost all of the sacred places, called huacas. Every so often a capac hucha ('royal obligation') festival was called by the priesthood. Scores of children would be sent to Cuzco for a blessing by the Inca ruler, then ritually married before returning home to be strangled, or killed by a blow to the head, or buried alive. It was a great honour to be chosen for sacrifice and victims were venerated.

1. Inca stonework, Cuzco. Although not neatly rectangular, the stone blocks fitted together with exceptional precision.

2. Like the ancient Egyptians, the Incas probably used timber rollers to transport stone blocks.

2

The Inca empire covered virtually the full range of South American landscape and climate, from high mountains to coastal desert and forested lowlands. With time, it might well have extended along the full length of the Andes, stretching northwards to embrace the independent gold-working cultures of the Muisca (or Chibcha) in the highlands of Colombia, and even the Tairona on the Caribbean coast. But in 1525, while visiting the northern limit of his empire with his warrior son Atahualpa, 2000 km (1200 miles) from his capital, the Inca Huayna Capac was struck down by disease. There had been news of strangely pale, bearded, fair-skinned people on the coast. Some said it was Viracocha (▷ p.76), returning from his sojourn in the Pacific. The disease proved fatal – it was smallpox. It had probably arrived with these strangers, and was equally ominous.

DOWNFALL

VERACRVZ N 2

1. A scene from the Conquest of Mexico, painted in the late 18th century, shows the conquistadors shortly after disembarkation. The Spanish horses, armour, weapons and sailing ships dumbfounded the Aztecs, and gave the conquistadors a tactical advantage that compensated for their small numbers.

enslavement against the Taino population. It brought one of the earliest public criticisms of their conduct from the Church, when in 1511 they were told that their unbridled cruelty had put them in a state of mortal sin. In 1492 there were probably over a million Taino on the island; by 1539 they had been almost completely eliminated.

The Spanish were on the trail of gold. A few expeditions gave them an inkling of what might lie on the mainland. In 1517 Fernandez de Córdoba found the first evidence of the Maya, plus some pieces of gold, on an island off the Yucatán Peninsula. The following year Diego Velásquez, governor of Cuba, dispatched another expedition to the mainland under his nephew Juan de Grijalva. He ran into hostilities from the Maya, but had more

friendly exchanges on the coast of northern Veracruz, and here he learned about the Aztecs. In 1518 the 33-year-old Hernán Cortés (1485–1547) won permission from Velásquez to take another expedition to the mainland. Almost immediately he came under suspicion of being interested only in personal gain, and an unreliable ambassador of Spain, but attempts to stall him failed.

To Tenochtitlán

Cortés left Cuba in February 1519 with 11 ships, 508 men, 16 horses and 10 cannon. After landing on the coast of the Gulf of Mexico, he stormed the town of Tabasco and was awarded the prize of slaves, including Malinche, a young woman who acted as his interpreter and became his mistress. Cortés then proceeded up the coast to Veracruz, where he announced that he was rejecting Velásquez's authority and would proceed on his own account. He then beached his ships to prevent any thought of retreat from his men. Cortés was greeted with a mixture of hostility and cautious welcome by the coastal peoples at the eastern extremities of the Aztec empire (▷ pp.63-9). They were fascinated by the Spanish horses, and were initially convinced that a horse and rider were one animal. Hearing of the great riches of Tenochtitlán, Cortés headed west on the 640-km (400-mile)

route into the highlands. Along the way, he won allies among the Totonacs, who were disenchanted by Aztec rule. Closer to Tenochtitlán, he fought with the Tlaxcalans and they, too, became allies.

Meanwhile, the Aztec emperor Montezuma II was paralysed by inaction. Cortés had arrived in the Aztec year One Reed, when, according to an ancient prophecy, the light-skinned, bearded god-king Quetzalcoatl would return from the east. Montezuma thought Cortés might be him. Other omens suggested calamity, which chimed with the Aztecs' fatalistic view of the world. Montezuma allowed Cortés and his growing army to approach

 BERNARDINO DE SAHAGÚN

The Catholic Church condemned the Aztec civilization as the work of the devil, but some of the missionaries sent to New Spain showed tolerance and sympathy towards its native peoples. Among them was Franciscan Friar Bernardino de Sahagún. He came to New Spain in the early days of the conquest and learned the Aztec language, Nahuatl. He then decided to produce a primer about Aztec life to assist missionaries in their work. So began his monumental investigation into the Aztec way of life – its history, religious beliefs, social structures, customs and practices. After 21 years (1547–68), Sahagún produced the 12-volume *Historia General de las Cosas de Nueva España* (General History of the Things of New Spain). A version of this work forms the Florentine Codex, and is a comprehensive source of information about the Aztecs. Scenes from the Florentine Codex are depicted on the right.

Tenochtitlán, and as they reached the shores of Lake Texcoco on 8 November 1517, he sent out a welcoming party, bearing gifts. The Spanish were invited to stay in the city. At first they were amazed by it. 'We were wonderstruck,' wrote Cortés's companion Bernal Díaz del Castillo. 'We said that what lay before us was like the enchantments told in ancient myths. Some of our soldiers even said that what we were seeing was a thing of dreams.' But they were appalled by the human sacrifice, which they condemned as the work of the devil. This aroused their instincts as warriors for Christ, and the rewards in booty were all too apparent.

Fearing that he would soon be expelled from Tenochtitlán, Cortés decided to secure his men's safety by taking Montezuma hostage. He made Montezuma swear allegiance to the Spanish king and demanded a ransom. But then a punitive mission from Spanish Cuba arrived on the coast of the Gulf, sent by Velásquez. Cortés rushed to the coast to head off this threat to his authority, captured the expedition's leader, persuaded many of its members to join him and set off back to Tenochtitlán with these reinforcements. In the meantime, growing tensions in Tenochtitlán between the Aztecs and the 200 Spanish left behind

1. The Spanish conquest of Mexico was illustrated in gory detail by contemporary Aztec artists. Here conquistadors, supported by their allies from Tlaxcala, attack Michoacán in western Mexico.

2. Portrait of Hernán Cortés by an anonymous artist. Reviled for his cruelties and distrusted as a leader, Cortés died a disappointed man in Spain in 1547, deeply resenting his country's lack of appreciation and gratitude for his achievements.

had triggered a violent confrontation, in which 100 Aztecs were killed. But when Cortés attempted to use Montezuma to quell the unrest, Montezuma's own people turned on their king and stoned him to death. The Spanish then suffered heavy losses as they were forcibly ejected from the city in what is called the Noche Triste ('sad night'), 30 June 1520.

Cortés regrouped his forces at Tlaxcala, then laid siege to Tenochtitlán. After a gruelling 93 days, on 13 August 1521, the city – dependent on supplies from outside – surrendered. Cortés immediately set about demolishing the monuments. With its central core destroyed, the Aztec empire collapsed. By 1526 Cortés was in control of the whole of Mexico, now renamed New Spain. As settlers and missionaries poured in, booty was shipped back to Spain, and to King Charles I (better known to history as the Holy Roman Emperor Charles V).

The native peoples of Mesoamerica were now subjected to a regime of great cruelty and intolerance, which was much criticized by a few missionaries, as well as by members of the government in Spain. But by far the greatest scourge was imported disease. Native American peoples had no immunity to smallpox, measles, whooping cough, influenza, or gastro-intestinal diseases, all of which were fatal and spread particularly rapidly in the towns and cities. In 1500 the native population of Mesoamerica had been somewhere between 11 and 25 million. By 1625 it had been reduced to 1.25 million. Despite the odds, pockets of resistance held out against Spanish conquest. The last rebels in the old Maya lands of Mexico were not subdued until 1901.

2

When Columbus landed in the New World in 1492, he mistakenly believed he had reached outlying islands of India or China. So he called the native people Indians, and the name has stuck.

THE LURE OF GOLD

Cortés's conquest of Mexico was the inspiration for the next great Spanish adventure. The conquistador Francisco Pizarro (*c*.1475–1541), veteran of the annihilation of the Taino on Hispaniola, knew well how a small body of men could overwhelm a whole nation if they were audacious enough to strike at its heart. Pizarro had heard rumour of the riches of South America and went into partnership with the soldier and explorer Diego de Almagro to fund an expedition in 1524–28. This first trip down the Ecuadorian coast came close to disaster, but it was during this period that the Inca ruler Huayna Capac appeared to contract smallpox and died (▷ p.77).

His death caused a dynastic split in the Inca empire. Huayna's son Huascar was appointed in Cuzco as his successor, but another son, Atahualpa, half-brother of Huascar, also claimed the throne from his base in Ecuador. The result was a bitter

1

 THE MYTH OF EL DORADO

Gold was the dream of the Spanish conquistadors and they were haunted by a story about a fabled city of gold, ruled by El Dorado, 'The Golden Man'. It led some explorers on a fruitless search across the Amazon Basin, others deep into the southwest of North America. The story may have derived from a custom carried out by the Muisca people of the highlands of Colombia. At the round volcanic Lake Guatavita, a new Muisca ruler would have gold dust blown over his clay-smeared body. Wearing only the gold dust and gold jewellery, he would be rowed into the middle of a lake on a gilded raft to make offerings to the gods by throwing gold and emeralds into the water. Efforts to dredge and drain the lake have continued into modern times, with only partial success.

1. Francisco Pizarro, a conquistador hardened by long experience in the New World, was 48 when he embarked on his conquest of the west coast of South America.

2. (opposite) An elaborate Chimú knife hilt is typical of the many thousands of gold artefacts that excited the greed of the conquistadors.

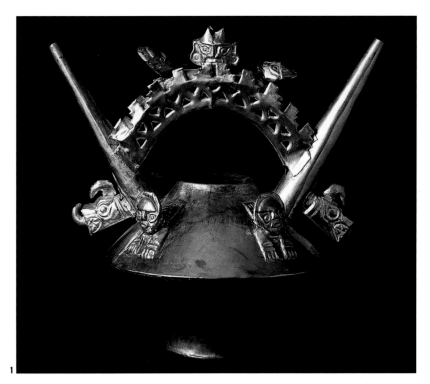

1

1. Lambayeque-style gold vase. Advancing towards Cajamarca in 1532, Pizarro's expedition passed through the Lambayeque valley, which had its own rich culture and distinctive art style.

2. A 16th-century engraving by Theodor de Bry expresses vividly the toil of Native American labourers commandeered to assist in the Spanish expeditions.

civil war, but Atahualpa gained the upper hand when he captured Cuzco and seized Huascar. At this point, in 1532, Pizarro returned to the Inca coast with 185 men and 37 horses. He pressed inland and contacted Atahualpa, who was with his army of 80,000 men outside the administrative centre of Cajamarca, 1000 km (600 miles) north of Cuzco. Atahualpa invited the Spanish to occupy the central square of the town and agreed to meet them next day. Certain of his own invincibility, Atahualpa arrived at dusk, carried on his royal litter and surrounded by 6000 retainers, all unarmed.

The Incas had not bargained for the duplicity of the Spanish, who had concealed themselves around the square. When Atahualpa arrived, he was given a prayer book, but could make no sense of it and threw it to the ground. At this point a friar turned and shouted, 'Come out, Christians! Come at these enemy dogs who reject the things of God!' The Spanish rushed from their hiding places on horseback, wielding their Toledo swords, while others opened fire with muskets. In the ensuing chaos, many thousands of Incas were massacred and Atahualpa was captured.

The end of the line

Atahualpa was held prisoner for eight months at Cajamarca by Pizarro, during which he continued to reign. He was convinced that the Spanish were just tribute hunters, and agreed to a huge ransom in gold and silver to secure his release. Meanwhile, he managed to have his brother Huascar assassinated, for fear that he would usurp him.

Atahualpa misunderstood Pizarro's motives: he wanted land and power as well as gold. For his part, Pizarro convinced himself that he could not release Atahualpa without the risk of losing power. So Atahualpa was tried and found guilty of inciting insurrection. On 26 July 1533, he was tied to a stake in the square of Cajamarca, and persuaded to accept Christianity so that he could avoid being burnt to death – which would have prevented him from having his body embalmed in the tradition of the Inca god-kings. Then he was garrotted.

With the elimination of Huascar and Atahualpa, the Inca empire collapsed and Pizarro became governor of Peru. He installed Manco Capac, brother of Huascar, as puppet ruler in 1534, but two years later Manco rebelled and established a final Inca dynasty in exile. It lasted until 1571, when his son Tupac Amaru was captured and beheaded.

Meanwhile, the new colonists had come to blows over the spoils of conquest. The conflict resulted in the execution of Diego de Almagro on the orders of Pizarro in 1538, and the revenge murder of Pizarro by supporters of de Almagro in 1541. Spanish explorers and missionaries fanned out across the continent in search of gold, land and slaves.

'INDIAN WARS'

In North America, the story was different, but no less tragic. The first European explorers to reach the continent, such as John Cabot in 1497, and Jacques Cartier in 1535, came in search of a route to the Far East. During the following century, the Portuguese, French, Spanish and English made unsuccessful attempts to settle, but it was not until 1607 that the first lasting settlement took hold, at the British colony of Jamestown, Virginia. This succeeded only with the help of the Algonkian people, led by Chief Powhatan, whose daughter Pocahontas married a leader of the colony, John Rolfe. The colony managed to survive because an export market in Europe was discovered for a new product – tobacco. But when more land was needed for plantations, this caused a dispute that

2   4

flared up into confrontation after Chief Powhatan's death. So began a cycle of offence, retaliation and resentment that was to underscore relationships with Native Americans throughout the history of their settlement. At the heart of the conflict lay incompatible attitudes to land: European settlers wanted to exploit it, own it, fence it in and control it; to the Native Americans, land was a gift from the creator, to be treated with respect, along with all the animals and produce that it furnished.

By the end of the 17th century there were 250,000 European settlers in North America, with the English on the east coast, the French along the St Lawrence River and around the Great Lakes, and the Spanish in eastern Florida, on the Gulf coast and in the southwest.

The tightening noose

In 1679 French explorer Robert de La Salle travelled from the Great Lakes to the Gulf of Mexico and claimed a huge swathe of central North America for France, naming it Louisiana after his king. In 1803 the USA bought this territory for $15 million.

When the United States devised its constitution in 1787, no provision was made for the Native Americans, although George Washington did propose humane coexistence. Government was always remote from the points of conflict. Bit by bit, settlers were pressing west, squatting on Native American lands, running into conflict and then demanding protection and retaliation from the government. Indian peoples closer to the east coast were seen as a problem in need of a robust solution.

1

1. The village of Pomeiock, 1587. This is one of a series of drawings by John White, governor of the failed English colony of Roanoke Island, North Carolina.

2. *Buffalo Hunt* by George Catlin, 1844. After 1830, Catlin, a Philadelphia lawyer, devoted his life to recording the vanishing way of life of the Plains Indians, and brought his exhibition to London in the 1840s.

2

In 1830, President Andrew Jackson managed to persuade Congress to pass the Indian Removal Act. This sanctioned the wholesale removal of eastern native peoples, such as the Cherokee, Creek, Chickasaw, Seminole and Choctaw, to lands beyond the Mississippi. When the Cherokee were forced to make the 1300-km (800-mile) journey in winter, 4000 died of exposure and starvation – a notorious episode known as the 'Trail of Tears'.

The Spanish, moving north from Mexico, began to settle the southwest of North America in the 17th century, spearheaded by Catholic missions. Their oppression led to the Pueblo Rebellion of 1680,

when the Spanish were ejected from Santa Fe and mission churches were burnt. It was almost 20 years before the missions returned. Fearing encroachment by North America and Russia, the Spanish set up their first mission in California in 1769.

In 1803 Captain Meriwether Lewis and Lieutenant William Clark led an expedition from the Mississippi to the Pacific coast to discover more about the little-known lands that lay between. This classic journey of US exploration revealed the vast riches of the West. Before long, wagon trains were cutting tracks along the Oregon, Mormon and Santa Fe trails, taking settlers to the west coast.

 DISCOVERING THE MAYA

The ruined cities of the Maya were unknown to the outside world until the mid-19th century, when they suddenly caught the public imagination. The cause of this turnaround was a collection of sketches by the English architect Frederick Catherwood (1799–1854), who accompanied the American lawyer John Lloyd Stephens (1805–52) on two expeditions to central America in 1839–40 and in 1841–2. Stephens' vivid accounts of their travels, together with Catherwood's images of temples covered by jungle, were highly popular and launched the serious study of the Maya ruins. For this reason, John Stephens is often said to be the 'discoverer of the Maya'.

The Californian Gold Rush of 1848 increased the traffic. Marauding Native Americans prompted the US army to restrict them to reservations by force. By 1860 they were surrounded from all sides.

In 1869 the Union Pacific and Central Pacific railroads were linked, uniting the two coasts of the USA across the Great Plains, and in the 1870s the buffalo herds were systematically wiped out in a campaign to undermine the Sioux people. By this time, the Plains Indians were in a state of open warfare, making a last-ditch stand against the US army sent to pacify them and herd them into reservations. At the Battle of Little Big Horn in 1876, chiefs Sitting Bull and Crazy Horse defeated forces under Lieutenant Colonel George Armstrong Custer. But it was the final triumph – Sitting Bull

1

1. Print of a Catherwood drawing of Izamal, Yucatán. Catherwood and Stephens were fascinated by the large stucco mask, a rare survivor of a common Maya architectural feature.

2. A contemporary lithograph of the Battle of Little Big Horn, 1876. The battle resulted from an effort to force the Sioux into reservations. Following a tactical misjudgement, Custer and his battalion of the Seventh Cavalry were wiped out to a man.

2

and Crazy Horse both died when supposedly resisting arrest. In December 1890 a party of 200 Sioux men, women and children was massacred at Wounded Knee, South Dakota, by the US army still seeking revenge. This tragic incident marked the close of the Indian Wars.

The ancient civilizations of the Americas had been overwhelmed by the Europeans – by their acquisitiveness, technological superiority and diseases. The surviving heirs to their impressive cultural legacy were reduced to a marginal existence – bit-players in the thrusting world of the modern Americas. Only since the latter part of the 20th century have they begun to regroup, and to reaffirm their legacy, while their conquerors meditate on their collective guilt and ponder what has been lost.

Meanwhile, the ruins of Teotihuacán, Moche ceramics, Maya temple sites, Inca goldwork and the broad spectrum of North American Indian crafts give tantalizing clues to the highly distinctive worlds that had evolved in the Americas during the 10,000 years or so when the two continents were allowed to follow their own destiny undisturbed.

FURTHER INFORMATION

BOOKS

Michael Coe, Dean Snow and Elizabeth Benson, *Atlas of the Ancient Americas* (Facts on File Inc., New York, 1980)
Covers all the Americas in one volume. A balanced and accessible introduction, well illustrated with maps, monuments and artefacts.

Elizabeth Baquedano, *Aztec* (Eyewitness Series, Dorling Kindersley, 1993)
A good children's introduction, with plenty of illustrated artefacts. Includes the Aztecs and ancient cultures of Mesoamerica and South America.

Claude Baudez and Sydney Picasso, *Lost Cities of the Maya* (New Horizons series, Thames & Hudson, 1992)
Focuses on the rediscovery of the Maya heritage from the 19th century onwards.

Serge Gruzinski, *The Aztecs: Rise and Fall of an Empire* (New Horizons series, Thames & Hudson, 1992)
A very readable introduction. Includes a section presenting original contemporary documents.

J.C.H. King, *First Peoples, First Contacts: Native Peoples of North America* (British Museum Press, 1999)
Excellent, heavily illustrated paperback volume to accompany an exhibition of artefacts, focusing on cultures at the point of contact with European explorers and settlers.

Colin McEwan, *Ancient Mexico* (British Museum Press, 1994)
Concise and approachable paperback, with good illustrations and an explanatory text covering the successive civilizations of Mexico.

Antony Mason, *Aztec Times* (If You Were There series, Marshall Publishing, 1997)
Heavily illustrated, large-format children's volume, providing an introduction to the Aztec way of life and mindset.

Richard F. Townsend (ed.), *The Ancient Americas: Art from Sacred Landscapes* (The Art Institute of Chicago, 1992)
Published in conjunction with a major exhibition of the same name, this beautifully illustrated, weighty volume contains authoritative essays and is full of fascinating insights.

MAGAZINE

National Geographic
The National Geographic Society takes great interest in American history and sponsors archaeological projects; issues regularly feature accessible and authoritative articles on the latest research and finds.

INDEX